CONTENTS

ALWAYS ROOM FOR IMPROVEMENT

For many years I juggled the pounds and the pennies to feed my family of four on a tight budget, and recently I had begun to feel that at last I had the economics under control and could relax. Our children had grown up and were settled in homes of their own, and I had to be resigned to cooking for just my husband and me again – a whole new ball game which, I confess, didn't come easy. I even decided this year, for want of some sort of challenge, that it was about time I began practising what it would be like to live only on a state pension so that it wouldn't come as so much of a shock to us when we do.

But in all this time I had never once given a thought as to how I would manage if I was on my own. So when various people, including the BBC, began asking me for ideas on how to cope on a limited income when you live alone, I decided – well, I only need a little prod to start me off – to have a go at that instead. Come to think of it, cooking for one is really the starting block. Get that bit right and cooking for more is bound to be easier and cheaper. If I could do it successfully I knew I wouldn't need to worry about growing old at all.

Most instruction books are written when the authors have got the answers right so there's nothing left to find out for yourself. This book is different. I have described an approach to cooking for one which worked very well for me, but – as my teacher was prone to say – there is still room for improvement. So once you've read the book, just think how much better you could do it yourself. I'd like *you* to be the one to put me right.

Shirley Goode
January 1987

4

I
THE CHALLENGE

Many years ago I didn't enjoy cooking at all. My early efforts always seemed to end up failures and I suppose I gave up trying too soon. (My husband says 'twice is always' where I'm concerned.) Gradually I came to rely more and more on ready-made and processed foods rather than take a chance on knocking something up from scratch. If you haven't much money you can't afford to make mistakes.

It wasn't until the money ran out altogether (my own fault – I was a bad manager too) that I was forced to make things to eat out of what I normally considered to be nothing of worth. I can still remember standing there alone in the kitchen saying out loud: 'I'm going to *have* to cope!' – but I didn't know how or where to begin.

Well, I started trying although even the most basic recipes seemed a nightmare and the kitchen was a disaster area for weeks. But I can't have done too badly for the family soon began to compliment me on the food and to ask why, all of a sudden, I had begun to serve better meals. They had never had it so good. The easy answer to that is: I had begun to think more about what I was doing and therefore to understand food a little better. Above all I stopped taking food for granted and began to discover its potential.

What fun it turned out to be. Not a lot of cookery books will tell you that, so I'm stressing the fact – find the right approach and you can have one heck of a good time, and this is true, I assure you, whether you're cooking for a family or only for yourself. There is absolutely no reason why, just because you live on your own, you shouldn't get the same enjoyment from shopping, cooking and eating that I do and not only manage but even save money in the process.

Self-imposed restrictions

Of course, it's one thing to write about the theory of cooking for one when you're assuming there are plenty of stores to draw upon or money is not too short. It's quite a different matter actually to live alone, relying only on a limited income with little in the cupboard. That's real life. So when the BBC approached me to look at cooking for one in the TV series *Bazaar*, I decided the only way to do it properly was to experience it for myself. And that is exactly what I did. I called it 'The Challenge': to live for four weeks on a small limited budget, cooking for and feeding just myself. (As it happened I was also called upon to entertain – more about that in Chapter 5.)

It wasn't meant to be easy. At least not at first. I planned to deny myself all normal sources of 'free' food (garden and hedgerow produce); foods from store (a godsend in the past); even freebies such as money-off coupons or reduced prices. I reckoned that if I could cope without all these, then when the opportunities came life could only get better.

Restrictions (self-imposed or otherwise) help me gain and keep control. The bigger the challenge, the greater the sense of achievement which gives such a good feeling that it's worth setting targets just for the fun of it.

My approach

Whenever I begin a new project I look for the best approach. It's easy to do something when you know you will enjoy doing it, and that means finding the right angle for *you*. I have to confess that, although normally you can't prise me out of the kitchen (except to play bridge – which these days has almost top priority), during those rare occasions when my husband has been away I've always made do with a snack rather than cook something. It never seemed worth the effort to prepare a proper meal just for me, and I know this is true of many people who live on their own.

This is because we always take more trouble over what we do for other people, and within the circle of our friends and family it's one of the ways we show our love for them. So it's not surprising we don't give ourselves the same attention.

For me, then, the best approach to 'The Challenge' was to make use of 'role-playing'. This I do when faced with a situation which I'd rather ignore. But can't.

Role-playing

Let's take housework as an example. I *hate* it. I always have and I probably always will. Even Shirley Conran can't make it easier for me. But sooner or later it *has* to be faced and the easiest and quickest way to get things back into shining order is for me to (literally) leave by my front door, switch roles and return by the back as 'my little treasure' (usually Hilda Ogden). Then – because I'm someone else – I see the place for what it is (a tip!) and do something constructive about putting it in order.

So – if, like me, you need a bit of help with the action when it comes to self-catering, imagine that you will be shopping and cooking for someone else, someone who lives on their own and who needs to eat proper nourishing meals. You could look upon yourself as their cook/housekeeper. Quite an important role – people get paid for doing that. But it's essential to switch back roles when it's time to eat because – who knows – your 'minder' might have role-played a *Cordon Bleu* cook and it would be a pity to miss that.

The day book

Because by nature I'm not an organised person I find it a great help to write things down. If you don't normally do this, why not have a go, jotting down hints, tips, good ideas, new recipes, how much things cost, how much you have saved, how you feel about things in general – and so forth.

Bits of paper get lost easily so each Christmas I ask for a page-a-day diary (it just looks more important – at a pinch an exercise book works just as well). One of my greatest pleasures is to read back over past years and see if this year I can do better. Here's an excerpt from January 1979 around the time when I first got into money difficulties and needed to find a solution:

1979   *January 8th*

Have to manage on v. little money. Food shortages in shops. Lorry drivers' strikes, high prices. But no matter, can't afford to buy anything anyway.
Check in freezer shows oddments that will have to make meals. Plenty of fish. Should be able to make 30 good meals plus extras – could spin out to 60 with care. Fair amount of dry goods in stock.
Family allowance will go on pocket money so will have to cope only on what I've got in store.

Well, I *did* cope (that's now history) but kept on writing it all down. Sometimes it was a recipe or two . . .

1982   *March 15th*

Bar-b-que sauce

2 tablespoons ketchup
2 tablespoons soy sauce
2 tablespoons marmalade
1 teaspoon Worcestershire sauce
1 tablespoon vinegar
1 tablespoon honey
1 teaspoon dry mustard

Mix all the ingredients together in a pan and bring to the boil. Baste pork spare ribs or spare rib chops with this while roasting them in the oven. (Or follow the directions opposite for chicken.)

Bar-b-qued chicken
Chicken thighs can either be cooked in the oven, grilled or
barbecued, so whether you're eating alone or having an *al
fresco* party keep this recipe in mind.

---

2 chicken thighs per person
Bar-b-que sauce (see opposite)

Remove the skin from the chicken thighs and slash the
flesh with a sharp knife. Place in a shallow dish and spoon
over the Bar-b-que sauce, turning the chicken to coat it
completely. Leave to stand for half an hour.
To cook in the oven: Place dish in a pre-heated oven at gas
mark 5, 275°F (190°C) and bake for 20 minutes, basting
once or twice with the juices.
To grill: Line the grill pan with foil. Brush the rack with oil
and grill the chicken for 7–8 minutes on each side,
brushing with more sauce for a crispy coating.
To barbeque: Brush the bars with oil and cook as for grilling.

Sometimes I began the year by writing down all the savings
I made. This example seems to come from a shop where I
sought out all the 'money-offs' before I did anything else.

1984   *January 9th*

Shopping savings (normal price in brackets):		saved (p)
Eggs (3 × 49)	3 × 18p	93
Nuts/raisins (£1.48)	98p	50
4 yogurts (54)	34p	20
Eggs (1 × 42)	1 × 18p	24
1 paté (reduced from 39p down to 29p, then 10p off that)	19p	10
12 oz (350g) mixed cooked meat pieces	97½p	60
6 oranges (16p ea.)	8p ea.	48
		£3.05

Doing-it-yourself also saves quite a bit as this muesli experiment shows. Of course, it was January again. Isn't it nearly always?

1984		January 24th
Work out muesli cost:	To buy: 1½lb (750g) costs 81p.	
My version:		
Wheat flakes	8oz (250g)	16p
Oat flakes	8oz (250g)	10p
Bran	3oz (75g)	5p
Dried fruit	2oz (50g)	6½p
Nuts	2oz (50g)	20p
Malt (Ovaltine)	½oz (15g)	3½p
	23½oz (690g)	61p
		Saves 20p

Other home-made goods (one month's supply):

Marmalade		£1.40 saved
Caster sugar		£0.16 saved
Icing sugar		£0.16 saved
Yogurt		£2.32 saved
Lemonade (elderflower)	at least	£2.00 saved
Bulk lager	at least	£16.00 saved
Muesli		£0.80 saved
		£22.84

This year my diary has been full of discoveries about my new project – feeding just me. I've jotted down notes, invented new recipes, spotted bargains, sorted out problems. Here are some of the first things I discovered.

The good and the bad

It soon became clear that there are both advantages and disadvantages to being single where food is concerned. The first snag is that it is always going to cost more to feed one person than (per head) two, three or more. Singles can't take advantage of economy packs if the contents won't be used up in a reasonable time or can't be shared with someone else. Individual portions are generally a more expensive way to buy.

But on the good side, the best thing about cooking for yourself is that you have no one else to please. You can, within reason, buy *your* favourite foods because there are no other palates to pander to. Mealtimes can fit in with social activities and, if you really don't feel hungry, then you haven't still got to prepare food for others. This I found to be sheer luxury.

What's more it really *can* be luxury. If you don't believe you can afford salmon or fillet steak on a restricted budget, then read on.

The budget

The amount of money you have to spend on food will vary a great deal from person to person. Some might feel deprived if they had less than £20 a week to spend while others can eat like kings spending only £10. Unfortunately some people have to manage on far less, and that's not so easy. But however much or little money you have, once you get the principal approach right you will get more for your money. This approach is the same whatever your income and you'll find a great deal more about this in Chapter 2.

I settled on a maximum expenditure of £15 for the first week of 'The Challenge' aiming to cut it by a third by the fourth week, and – what's more important – keep it at that level from then on. Would I be able to do it? I really didn't know, but I intended to have a darn good try.

2
THE KNOWLEDGE

Recently I read a fascinating book by Maud Pember Reeves called *Round About a Pound a Week* (Virago, 1979) describing a social study which took place in the early part of this century. A group of women living on a very low income were asked to record in detail what happened to their money each week. It was normal in those times for the husband to hand over all his wage to his wife who would then settle the dues. These were pretty standard in all the homes – high on the list would be the rent, of course, then fuel, clothing and cleaning materials (not so much for personal use, more to keep up appearances with clean curtains and donkeystoned doorsteps). Also, because the diet was inadequate and the standard of health low, many children died in infancy so some money had to be paid each week into a funeral fund.

Because of fixed ideas and traditions food did not have top priority. There was not a lot of money left over for it anyway. When they could afford meat it was Dad as the breadwinner who had to have it. It was important that he at least be strong enough to work. Mum and the kids made do with scraps from the joint, potatoes (always potatoes), suet pudding or bread and scrape.

But one woman – on exactly the same income – managed famously. Before marriage she had worked as a cook and obviously knew what she was about. With a happy husband and children bright-eyed and bushy-tailed she did not need to pay out on burial insurance. She had the Knowledge.

Several decades later, during the last war, everyone got it right. Although most food was rationed and meagre by today's standards it was adequate and nutritious (all credit going to the Ministry of Food who worked out the perfect balance). Every individual (give or take a pregnant woman) had exactly the same basic food allowance and it was up to them (or the family cook if she hadn't gone to work on the buses) to do what they could with it.

Just imagine what it would be like today if you were only allowed one egg a fortnight! No wonder that the housewife – who at the start often didn't know the difference between a calorie and a carbohydrate – had become very resourceful and ingenious by the end of the war and had learned more about nutrition than most of us know today.

I particularly remember one dreadful wartime day when I was holding The Egg in one hand while reaching for a cup with the other. My father, who was nearby, gave a tremendous sneeze which so startled me that I clutched the egg tight, trying to cling to the wall at the same time. The next few minutes were chaotic while Dad and I tried to rescue as much egg as possible by carefully scraping it off the wall, off me, off anywhere it had hit, and collecting it into the cup so that Mum could still use it. Nothing was ever wasted.

By the end of the war, because everyone had been eating the right foods and not a lot else, we had become healthier as a nation than ever before, and many good tips and recipes which originated in those austere times are still popular today. For instance, it took a war to make offal acceptable and here are a few smashing recipes (circa 1940) which make the most of a little liver. Quantities, naturally, are for one.

Liver aiguillettes

3–4oz (75–125g) pig's liver
1/2 beaten egg (see p.25)
1 slice of bread, crumbed
Sunflower oil

Cut the liver into thin strips. Dip into the egg, then the breadcrumbs (at a pinch you could use seasoned flour) and then shallow-fry in hot oil. Serve with a crisp salad.

Liver casserole

3–4oz (75–125g) pig's liver
Seasoned flour
Sunflower oil
1/2 small onion, grated
1 small turnip, peeled and sliced
1 carrot, sliced
2oz (50g) long-grain rice
1 teaspoon brown sauce
8fl oz (250ml) water

Cut the liver into slices and dip in the seasoned flour. Fry for a couple of minutes in hot oil, turning once.

Place the liver, prepared vegetables, rice and sauce in a small casserole and pour in the water. Cover and cook in the oven at gas mark 4, 350°F (180°C) for 45 minutes.

Liver with stuffing

1 slice of bread, crumbed
1 dessertspoon grated onion
Pinch dried sage or mixed herbs
Pepper
1–2 teaspoons beaten egg (see p.25)
3–4oz (75–125g) pig's liver
2 bacon rashers

First make the stuffing by mixing together the breadcrumbs, onion, dried herbs and pepper to taste. Bind together with the beaten egg and a little water if necessary. Slice the liver thinly and lay in a baking tin. Spread the stuffing over the liver and top with the bacon. Pour in 2 tablespoons water or stock and bake at gas 3 or 4, 325–350°F (170–180°C) for 30 minutes.

Variation: I like to form the stuffing into 'sausages' which I then roll up in the liver. Place these side by side in the baking-tin with enough liquid to come half-way up the rolls. Top with bacon and bake as above.

Convenience foods

After the war came a time to relax and try to forget all about austerity. Along came convenience foods and the liberated female so it was not surprising that we were easily persuaded to do anything but ration our eating and were won over to the idea that it really was so much better for us to let the manufacturers do most of the work. The food industry boomed.

More and more people ate less and less fresh food, turning instead to the convenience foods which are often so processed and additive-packed that they bear little resemblance to the original ingredients. We rely on these today to such an extent that many people wouldn't recognise a pea-pod if they saw one. Have we got our priorities wrong again? Have we lost the Knowledge?

I can hear some low protests from some of you at this point. Surely, you mutter, if you're a single person who goes out to work, or an elderly person without a lot of energy, doesn't it make sense to take the load off your shoulders? If you can buy something wholly or partly prepared why bother to start from the beginning. Surely *some* convenience foods are a good buy?

The short answer to that is: Yes. But do you know which? I honestly didn't until I began to do some checking. The easy way to find out is next time you bring home a convenience pack read what's printed on it. Then make it from scratch and cost out the result. You'll probably find, as I did, that quite a lot of things can just as quickly and easily be made at home – and far more cheaply. On the

15

other hand some things break even cost-wise and if they save time and you are happy with the ingredients (remember the additives) and can stomach the flavour – well then, why not? But be very selective. Make it *your* personal choice. Don't be swayed by advertising.

Take beefburgers, for instance. So easy, isn't it, to slip a pack of frozen ones in your shopping basket? But look at these calculations of mine:

Cost to buy 1lb frozen burgers (80% minimum beef):

4 × 4oz packs (i.e. 8 × 2oz burgers) @ 49p per pack
Total cost = £1.96p (approx 25p per 2oz burger)

2 × 8oz pack (i.e. 4 × 4oz burgers) @ 79p per pack
Total cost = £1.58p (approx 40p per 4oz burger)

This first lot of sums showed me you get better value, ounce for ounce, if you buy the larger burgers, i.e. the quarterpounders.

But now compare the cost with home-made.

Pkt ingredients	Home ingredients	Cost (p)
Beef	13oz (375g) *best* minced beef	121
Onion	1oz (25g) onion, grated	1
Rusk	1 slice bread, crumbed	2
Vegetable protein	1 egg (animal protein)	7
Flavouring	Dash brown sauce	1
Spices	Pepper	½
Salt, flavour enhancer, preservative, polyphosphates }	Not used	
		‾‾‾
		132p

The above quantity makes either 8 × 2oz burgers @ 16½p each or 4 × 4oz 'quarterpounders' @ 33p each. (Had I used 'standard' mince @ 98p per lb as against the better quality mince @ £1.40p I could have reduced the overall cost from £1.32p to 91p – but then standard mince can be rubbish!)

And are burgers a time-consuming fiddle to make? Not at all. Just put all the ingredients in a large bowl and mix them thoroughly together. Divide the mixture into 4 or 8 balls, depending on what size you want them to be, and toss them in a little seasoned flour. Press each ball into a flat cake and shallow-fry in hot oil, turning once. Alternatively, if you have the oven on you can bake them on a greased tray at gas mark 5, 400°F (200°C) for about 20 minutes. It's well worth making up the quantity given above and freezing the uncooked burgers, but if you don't have a freezer just use 3oz (75g) beef, 1 teaspoon grated onion, 1 teaspoon breadcrumbs, 1 tablespoon beaten egg and a little seasoning for one portion. (Don't forget you can freeze burgers in the ice-making compartment of most fridges as long as you use them up within three days.)

I find it helps to keep a record of these sort of comparison costings because there's nothing like words on paper in black and white to show things as they really are. Here are a few more examples from my day book:

White sauce: *mix v. home-made.*

Packet mix: *costs 16p. But then I am expected to add ½ pint (300ml) milk. Real cost: 28p*
Home-made: *¾oz (20g) flour (1p), ¾oz (20g) butter (4½p), seasoning (½p), a little onion (optional: 2p), ½ pint (300ml) milk (12p). Total cost: 20p*
Using dried milk/water and concentrated butter reduces the cost to 13p.
Making-up time: *using a roux (see p. 18) – the same.*

Madeira Cake: *mix v. home-made.*

Packet mix: *costs 35p. Add 1 egg/water. Real cost: 42p.*
Home-made: *4oz (125g) flour (4p), ½ teaspoon baking powder (1p), 2½oz (65g) butter (15p), 2½oz (65g) sugar (3½p), 1½ eggs (10½p), 3 tablespoons milk (2p), grated lemon rind (3p). Total cost: 34p*
Making-up time: *Quicker to use mix; also quicker to cook.*

17

Pancake Batter: *mix v. home-made.*

Packet mix: *costs 39p. Add water. Real cost: 39p*
Home-made: *8oz (250g) flour (8p), 2 eggs (14p), 1 pint (600ml) milk (24p). Total cost: 46 p*
   Using dried milk/water reduces cost to 34p.
Making-up time: *About the same. Good value and useful if you only need a small amount of batter: just measure out the amount you need.*

Roux

This is a mixture of equal quantities of flour and butter which are worked together very thoroughly and then formed into a pat to be kept in the fridge to use as required. Some flours seem to thicken more than others but a good rule of thumb is to allow 1 ½oz (40g) roux to thicken ½ pint (300ml) of liquid, e.g. milk for a basic white sauce, or chicken or fish stock for velouté sauce.

   To use, just drop small pieces of roux into the warm liquid, stirring constantly and heating gently until the mixture boils and thickens to the consistency you require. Season to taste.

What to buy?

'So,' I hear you asking, 'What foods should I buy?' Well, as few convenience foods as possible apart from those you definitely know to be good value. There are ways of making up your own time-savers (see pp. 83–85). But when it comes to fresh food I don't intend to be dogmatic. We've all got different tastes and I'd much rather you chose what you want rather than what I think you should.

   The important thing is the *balance*. Aim to have something from the three basic food groups at each meal: protein (mainly animal foods, but also pulses and nuts), vitamins and minerals (vegetables, fruit, cereals, dairy food) and carbohydrates (cereals, sugar, fat).

Vitamins and minerals can vary from food to food. Here's a good way to remember some of them – *colour coding*.

Orange and red:
Vitamin A
  Oranges, carrots, apricots, tomatoes.

Brown:
Vitamin B
  Liver, wholewheat bread, cocoa, yeast extract.

Iron
  Beef, kidney, liver, curry powder, cocoa, dried apricots, prunes.

Green and yellow:
Vitamin C
  Brussels sprouts, cabbage, lettuce, green peppers, parsley, new potatoes, lemons, grapefruit, bananas.

White:
Calcium
  Fish, milk, onions, nuts.

Carbohydrate
  Potatoes, parsnips, pasta, pulses, sugar, bananas, rice.

You'll note the gaps. Why haven't I mentioned blackcurrants (high in vitamin C) and eggs (rich in iron). Well actually they just don't fit into the colour chart, so use this only as a guide. To find out more you can't do better than read *The Manual of Nutrition* published by HMSO (1985). Don't be put off by the title. It's a very easy and enlightening read.

☆ *You absorb more iron from food if you take it with some vitamin C. Example: a drink of orange juice with your breakfast egg.*

We don't normally think of our meals as 'fuel' and rarely count up the grams of protein or the vitamins we chomp through each week. So it is possible that you are taking in too much (expensive and unnecessary) or not enough (unhealthy). To make it easy I've devised this approach – the Rule of Four – which not only helps sort out the budget and nutrition in one go, but also, within its limitations, leaves everyone free to buy mainly what they fancy.

Rule of Four

This really does work like magic and as well for one person as for a large family. It's very simple to do and after you've tried it for a while you'll find – as I did – that enough rubs off so that you can go back to random shopping if you want to – but with more awareness. A discipline like this is not meant to be used all the time, although it can be. Look upon it as a type of challenge that puts your shopping into perspective. Whether or not you need to save money try it anyway, then, if it ever does come to the pinch, you will know you really can cope.

What you do is divide your food budget into four and allocate one quarter to each of the following sections:
1 *Meat/fish*
2 *Dairy*
3 *Fruit/vegetables*
4 *Groceries.*

Previously I'd always worked on the theory that if I bought some fresh foods and took advantage of all the offers going, hoping to fill my shopping trolley before the money ran out, I'd be bound to have enough. It never occurred to me that I could be buying too much . . . of the wrong things.

Whether or not you wish to change your modus operandi it's not a bad idea to list what you have been doing to date. For one week jot down everything you buy together with its weight and cost, and include anything taken from the storecupboard. One friend who tried this was shocked when she realised how much bread and cakes (not to mention biscuits) she was buying and eating – so did something about it. Another realised she was eating a lot of protein but not much 'vegetation'. Slight adjustments not only made them both feel healthier and happier (if you have the first you get the second as a gift), but they both had more money left in their pockets.

The next week try the Rule of Four. Obviously you should avoid high prices so that you can buy as much as you can with the money available. (Price has very little to do with food value anyway – did you know the humble mackerel is much more nutritious than the glamorous sole?) But don't spend all your allowance on each section if you don't need to. Begin with one of the first three sections and buy the groceries last and see how it works out. You can read in Chapter 3 what I bought with my budget but everyone's tastes are different so do look on my choices as examples not instructions!

Spreading the load

Once the week's supplies have been safely gathered in, then you can plan a menu. (Yes, do this even though there's only you.) It's far cheaper to sort out what meals you're going to cook *after* you've had a chance to pick the bargains rather than make decisions before you shop.

Plan your balanced meals (an expression I hate but I can't think of a better one) in the form that you like best. A helping of protein doesn't always mean meat, the main meal could be a fish dish or something made with eggs and milk (a pudding perhaps). Or it could be a dish composed mainly of vegetable protein: nuts, pulses and grain. Or a bumper cheese and salad sandwich. The best thing about our food is that we can have it in such *variety*.

How to make recipes work for one

A good meal is one presented to stimulate every one of our five senses: Sound (le Crunch), Taste (yummy), Smell (aah . . . Bisto), Touch (ouch it's *hot*), and Sight (looks good enough to eat).

It's generally the latter sense that first inspires us to make a dish. We may not have tried it before, we probably don't know what's in it, but we *do* like the look of it. One glance at a photograph in a magazine or recipe book and our mouths begin to water.

This is usually due to the skills of someone called a food stylist – someone who knows a great deal about the importance of presentation and although by law he or she must follow the recipe to the letter, a stylist is nevertheless quite capable of substituting many ingredients and still making the dish look much the same. I know because I've worked as a stylist myself – but that's another story.

Take a tip from the stylist and remember that most recipes are very adaptable once you understand what they are trying to achieve. If it's a savoury dish then ask yourself if it is just a variation on a theme. Would it really matter if you changed a couple of ingredients, or even all of them? For instance, although it's usually a certain combination of meat, vegetables and seasonings that gives a casserole its character and name, there's no reason on earth why you can't vary it. Although *osso buco* is traditionally made with veal, it's just as good made with lamb. Smoked mackerel pâté made with butter, cream and lemon juice can just as easily be made with margarine, yogurt and vinegar. And, for that matter, herring or sardines instead of mackerel.

Smoked mackerel pâté

3oz (75g) smoked mackerel, skinned
1oz (25g) margarine
1 teaspoon vinegar
1 tablespoon thick yogurt
Pepper to taste

Flake the fish, soften the margarine and pound the two together in a bowl (use the end of a wooden spoon). Mix in the vinegar and yogurt. Season to taste. The mixture should be smooth. (If you have a liquidiser or food processor just put all the ingredients in together and whizz for a few seconds until well blended.)

Cover and chill for at least 1 hour. Serve with toast, crackers or pitta bread (p.92). Store in the fridge. Keeps up to 3 days.

It is rare that you will have all the right ingredients in the house for every recipe that you want to follow, but, bless their hearts, cookery writers are almost as persuasive as the manufacturers and we're forever trotting out to buy that extra couple of ounces of something which is not actually crucial to the dish. And then control in the kitchen goes flying out of the window. So always try and get away with what you've got – here are some do's and don'ts to help you.

Unnecessary in **most** recipes
- Exact amounts of meat or vegetables.
- Self-raising flour – use plain and add baking powder. To each 8 oz flour add:
  1 level teaspoon for fruit (rich) cakes
  2 level teaspoons for plain cakes and sponges
  4 level teaspoons for scones
- Fresh milk – use dried milk powder and water.
- Raisins – use sultanas, currants, chopped dried fruit, or vice versa.
- Specific types of pulses – most are interchangeable but watch out for different cooking times.
- Specific types of pasta – again, most are interchangeable.
- Breadcrumbs for coating – use crushed cornflakes or cream crackers.

Necessary in **most** recipes.

A good rule of thumb is to ask yourself *why* a particular ingredient is used. If you can't think of a substitute that does the same job then it's necessary. These are the most common essential 'jobs':

Raising agents: These are added to a mixture (usually containing flour) to make it lighter and more open in texture. Baking powder is good for general use in baking but bicarbonate of soda can be substituted if the mixture contains an acid (i.e. buttermilk or yogurt). Yeast when used with strong flours produces a bread-like texture, but it can be used in cakes. When stiffly beaten egg whites incorporate air into a mixture. The trick is then to *fold* them gently into the mixture. Too heavy handling and the whole lot collapses.

Setting agents: These make things 'jell' and become what I call 'cuttable'. They include eggs and gelatine. Try to avoid boiling gelatine as this will reduce its setting quality. Dissolve it instead in warm water. 1 teaspoon of gelatine crystals will set ¼ pint (125 ml) liquid.

Binding agents: Quite simply these hold ingredients together and prevent them separating, e.g. water in pastry, egg in beefburgers.

Fats: These range from butter through margarine, lard, suet and dripping to oils. They are used for frying and baking and are interchangeable to a certain extent, though each has its own flavour and character. Avoid using the saturated animal fats in favour of the polyunsaturated ones such as sunflower and safflower margarine and oil.

Cakes and desserts, in particular, tend to have ingredients and proportions carefully balanced and it's not a good idea to experiment too much unless you can stand the loss. (You learn a great deal by experimenting though.) Nevertheless, keeping the same measurements you can often substitute one type of flour for another, or one type of fat for another, and definitely change a flavouring.

Converting amounts

Most cookbooks are written for family eating – this means four portions (but do check). Even cookery books written especially for one tend to include recipes which will feed two on the assumption that you won't mind eating the other half the next day.

I think this has something to do with the egg. Even a family recipe sometimes only uses one. Have you ever seen a recipe that gives half an egg in its list of ingredients? In this book you will.

☆ *One whole grade 2 egg will, when beaten, measure out to four tablespoons.*
One grade 2 yolk only will measure out to four teaspoons. (See also Chapter 4.)

To convert a family recipe for four into a single portion you obviously need to divide the weights and measures by four. It helps me when doing this to see it as a fraction: the full weight on top, with the four (portions) below:

3oz becomes 3 over 4 = ¾
so ¾oz is what you will need.

When the top number is larger than the bottom you still write it the same way:

11oz becomes 11 over 4 = 11¼
Divide the bottom number into the top number – this then becomes 2¾. So you need 2¾oz.
(Of course, if you're clever enough to work in metric this doesn't apply. Just divide the grams in the normal way and well done!)

Whenever you convert a family recipe to one serving, pencil in the new weights so you don't have to work them out each time.

Chicken hot-pot

This is my adaptation and conversion of a family recipe to single-portion dimensions as an example of how you can juggle around with ingredients to end up with a very good dish similar to, but not exactly the same as the original. In other words: use what you've got.

Original ingredients	Adaptation for One
1 lb 4oz (625g) chicken, jointed	2 chicken thighs
8oz (250g) each leeks, carrots, turnips (²⁴/₄oz)	6oz (175g) mixed vegetables (carrot, celery, onion or whatever)
4oz (125g) streaky bacon (⁴/₄oz)	1oz (25g) bacon bits
4oz (125g) mushrooms	–
1 tablespoon oil	1 dessertspoon sunflower oil
1oz (25g) butter	–
10fl oz (300ml) chicken stock and 5fl oz (150ml) red wine (¹⁵/₄fl oz)	4fl oz (115ml) chicken stock
	–
4oz (125g) barley flakes (⁴/₄oz)	1oz (25g) pearl barley
Bouquet garni	Pinch mixed herbs

Wipe the chicken pieces with kitchen paper. Trim the vegetables and slice, chop or dice them. De-rind the bacon, wipe the mushrooms (if used).

Heat the oil/butter in a casserole and fry the chicken pieces for 5 minutes. Remove and set aside. Add the vegetables and bacon and cook over a low heat until the onions (leeks) are tender. Add stock, (wine), herbs, (mushrooms) and barley. Stir well. Return the chicken pieces to the pan and bring to the boil. Reduce the heat and simmer for 30 minutes, stirring from time to time.

Many scales can't cope with tiny amounts so it's worth investing in a set of measuring spoons. Make up your own chart as to which spoons will hold ½oz (15g), ¾oz (20g) or 1oz (25g) of different things – flour, sugar, rice, etc.

I used to crave for the old-fashioned balance scales but recently I've been won over to a far more sophisticated and accurate version. Electronic (battery driven) and not cheap – but worth saving up for – it weighs to the quarter ounce, converts from imperial to metric at the touch of a button and *then*, after you've punched in a code, can tell you the calories, fats and carbohydrates of whatever it is you are weighing. It even switches itself off when you forget. Magic. I admit you'll shudder when you see the price of these, but the ordinary type of spring scales are not nearly so accurate, and if you regularly have to weigh out small amounts you are probably using more than you need. It all mounts up.

Company policy

Eating is usually thought of as a pleasurable activity and a way of socialising, rather than just as a means of keeping alive. If you used to cook for a family and are now on your own you probably find it hard to maintain an interest in cooking. But you don't always *have* to be alone. Why not entertain occasionally? Try sharing: you go to Cynthia's on Thursdays, she comes to you each Tuesday. Cooking for two is marginally cheaper than cooking for one so you both benefit. In more ways than one.

Sometimes, because a portion *looks* small and probably takes only a few minutes to eat (if that) our mind tells us that we are still hungry. This has got nothing to do with the nutritional side at all. Most of us need to gnaw away off and on (not all the time) for about twenty minutes before we feel satisfied. So chewing everything

27

thirty times makes a lot of economical sense – never mind the digestion question. With a friend to share a meal you'll probably find you spend half the time talking. Moral: portions need not be large.

Portion padding

If false hunger keeps striking, aim to present yourself with a meal that gives the appearance of a plateful even if it starts out only covering a saucer. There's a lot you can do with good honest air and a bit of elbow grease. Incorporate as much as possible by slicing thinly, shredding, grating and whisking. Raw vegetables prepared in this way seem to take *ages* to eat – and they are good for you too. Try these combinations of lovely crunchy things.

Coleslaw

The simplest coleslaw is just finely shredded white cabbage tossed in a salad dressing. By adding more raw vegetables (or fruit) you can vary the appearance and flavour.

Try these for size, allowing a total amount of about a cupful as an accompaniment to a main dish:

Cabbage/celery/apple
Cabbage/carrot/onion
Chinese leaves/carrot/celery
Carrot/apple
Carrot/celery

Dressings:
Either use mayonnaise (p.97), mayonnaise with yogurt, yogurt with a touch of honey, or vinaigrette.

Vinaigrette dressing

2–3 tablespoons sunflower oil
1 tablespoon lemon juice or vinegar
1/2 teaspoon mustard powder
Pepper, just a pinch of white or a grind of black

Put all the ingredients into a screw-top jar and shake until
well blended. It will keep in the fridge for a few days, but
tastes better made up fresh.

As an alternative to a large plateful try serving yourself
several small courses. Have a 'luxury' starter to cheer you
up followed by a very plain main course and a cheap but
cheerful dessert. Read through the section on entertaining
(pp.105–119) to get some ideas.
   Don't forget the importance of fibre. This really is
satisfying. One jacket potato is incredibly filling with the
fibre mainly in the skin . . . the bit we all too often throw
away. When I'm feeling really thrifty I make one potato do
the work of two by first baking it and then removing the
flesh. This is kept for one dish (see below) while I pile a
savoury filling into the shell as another. This one is a
favourite:

Frijoles refritos with salad
Crisp green salad with re-fried beans

½oz (15g) bacon fat
1 dessertspoon onion, finely grated
3 tablespoons cooked red kidney beans or tinned baked beans
1 fresh or canned tomato, skinned and chopped
Pinch chilli powder
Pepper to taste

Melt the fat in a frying-pan and lightly fry the onion. Add
the beans, heat through and mash well. Stir in the tomato,
chilli powder and seasoning. Mix well. Simmer until the
mixture is fairly dry.
   Half-fill a baked potato shell with shredded crisp
lettuce and cucumber. Top with the hot bean mixture. An
optional finish (but good) is a sprinkling of grated cheese.

I can foresee the day when an enterprising manufacturer,
realising the potential of this, will start marketing frozen

cooked potato skins to fill yourself. But you'll be one step ahead, won't you?

Now what about that scooped-out potato . . .?

Fish pie with potato crust

This is the type of dish which can partly or wholly be made with left-overs. *Planned* leftovers, of course – that goes without saying!

6oz (175g) cooked flaked fish
1 hardboiled egg, chopped
6oz (175g) cooked carrots, diced
1 tablespoon fresh parsley, chopped (optional but worth it)
5fl oz (150ml) velouté sauce (white sauce made with stock instead of milk)
6–8oz (175–250g) mashed potato
A little butter
Pepper

Grease an ovenproof pie dish. Spread the fish evenly in the dish with the egg and scatter over the carrots. Stir the parsley into the sauce and spoon over the fish mixture. Cover with the mashed potato, dot with butter and season with a shake of pepper. Cook in the oven at gas mark 6, 400°F (200°C) for 20 minutes until the potato is crisp and brown.

Get out of old habits

Although potatoes are a good and nutritious food, prices sometimes rocket due to crop failure. In this country the potato is looked upon as one of our staple foods and for years I used to serve potatoes every day with the main meal (chips being the favourite). Then in 1976 came a bad year with very high potato prices – I just couldn't afford to keep buying them. So I started to use alternatives.

We got so fond of the rice, pasta and pancake dishes which are the staple foods of other countries that we never returned to the daily spud, treating it more as a proper vegetable to be served occasionally in the way we liked best: sometimes chips (now oven variety – not deep-fried), normally in its jacket, but never just plain boiled unless they are lovely new potatoes in their skins.

So don't feel pressured to buy a 'staple' food when the price goes up just because it's what you usually eat. There will always be something else cheaper and just as tasty. Go on – broaden your horizons.

The storecupboard
Did you know that practically all we need nutritionally can be found in what we call 'dry goods', the only other essential being water? Not an ideal way to live but useful to know. Even fresh vitamin-packed plant life can be had when you've a packet of mung (or similar) beans to sprout. So building up a useful storecupboard had to be part of my plan for my four-week experiment.

My memories of storing food begin in wartime when my mother kept several boxes full of tinned food under my bed. These were very precious items only to be opened at Christmas and on birthdays. More tins were kept under the stairs and one of my most vivid recollections is of sheltering there during a daylight air raid (we lived in Coventry) and my mother moving every tin on the shelves down to floor level 'so they won't fall on your head when the bombs drop'. I think what she actually meant was so that they wouldn't get dented on my head . . .

It's not surprising then that I grew up believing that food in store was an essential part of housekeeping. The trouble was that once I had my own home and saved to put the tins and packets on the shelves I'd go out and buy something else to eat. I was like a squirrel, hoarding for emergencies.

It was perhaps as well I did for when money did run short I was able to use up all my stock of tinned foods, but when *they'd* gone I was forced to do what I could with the very basics that were still there and I discovered that these were really the important ones:

- flour for pastry, pasta, cakes, bread;
- rice for puddings and savouries;
- oatmeal for porridge, biscuits and to grind up for flour;
- gelatine as a setting agent;
- herbs and spices for flavouring;
- dried apricots for puddings and pie-fillings;
- dried milk to supplement the fresh.

It didn't take me long to appreciate the value of my 'stores' and I began using them regularly to supplement the fresh foods instead of hoarding them. Most of the tinned fruit and vegetables were never replaced, the only canned foods still allowed space being tomatoes, tomato purée, sardines and, occasionally, baked beans. I bought and used more pulses and grains which led to a wider variety of meals. I hardly ever use salt now, finding herbs, spices and vegetables such as celery healthier substitutes.

Savoury rice

Personally I find plain boiled white rice a bit bland so I often add a little something. One way to do this is to cook it in water to which you've added lemon juice (see lemon shell tip, p.60) or orange juice. Both go well with chicken and fish. Add extra crunch with a dessertspoon of peanuts, a few (frozen) peas, or half an ounce of sultanas. Alternatively cook the rice in beef or chicken stock.

However, if you wish to keep some cooked rice for another dish cook only in plain water, drain well and keep the extra in the fridge for no more than 24 hours.

3
STARTING FROM SCRATCH

I started 'The Challenge-to-Feed-One' in early summer, but because it had been a severe and prolonged winter there wasn't as much fresh produce around as there should have been and none of it seemed cheap. Nevertheless, working to the Rule of Four with my weekly budget of £15 I had a generous £3.75p to spend on each of the four food sections. Looking at it that way it did seem quite a lot. I was sure I would be able to manage. But I hadn't really appreciated the amount of groceries that I was going to need to buy at the start of the first week. Quite a lot of things are normally scattered around my kitchen always ready to hand and usually taken for granted – herbs, spices, cooking oil, vinegar, tea. This time they wouldn't be there. And they all cost money.

It seemed the only way I would be able to buy all these things and more was to remember that although I could spend £3.75 each time I didn't *have* to, and – as long as I kept my sights firmly fixed on the lower price range – I probably wouldn't *need* to. As long as I made sure to buy enough fresh foods first, any money left over could go towards those extra groceries I needed to start me off. That was the theory anyway. How about the practice?

Keeping a record

I tried hard to keep accurate notes as I shopped and I suggest you do the same. Then you will know which area you saved money in and be able to plan next week's shopping accordingly. The record I made of what I had bought doubled as a shopping reminder for me the following week and, more importantly, acted as a guide for comparing price and weight. You really do need an on-the-spot reference to find the best value for money.

☆ *Try to keep your basic stores close at hand, preferably in lidded glass jars on your worktop. Remember that out of sight is out of mind. Being able to see things constantly reminds you to make use of them.*

The shopping

My shopping plan was this: at the beginning of the first week I would buy all the food in one go at the supermarket and pay full prices, i.e. not taking any advantage of offers going. This once-a-week shop can be very convenient for the single person who goes out to work and who just can't spare the time to traipse around different stores. On the other hand, the more chance you have to shop around, the more likely you are to pick up a bargain. Swings and roundabouts.

The second week would be a repeat of the first, with the same things being bought, but this time I planned to take advantage of any special offers going to find out how much difference they could make.

But not everybody lives near a supermarket and older people can't usually carry a week's shopping in one go. Single parents may have to manage an errant toddler and will probably find a couple of short trips easier and more practical. So the third week I decided I would buy most things locally in the smaller shops – butcher, baker, candlestick maker – to find out if I could do better, or worse.

The fourth week would be a hotch-potch, trying to get the best from all worlds.

What I bought

Although one week's shopping would obviously include all four sections I've split these up in this chapter, keeping each section separate so that it is easier for you to compare and for me to chat about. You'll notice that gradually I was able to introduce more variety into my purchases, although some foods cropped up week after week for reasons of comparison. I was able to stockpile stores yet the money held up well. In fact, by week 4 I *was* able to cut my expenditure overall by a third, something I'd hope for but not quite expected to achieve.

All this cash in hand meant that in future my eyes could occasionally light upon that fillet steak and salmon I told you about earlier and know that now and again I'd be able to afford them. Perhaps even once a month. But only so long as I took great care at other times. You can afford almost anything if you really *try*. But of course there are plenty of very reasonably priced foods around which are just as good to eat – it all boils down to what you do with what you've got.

FISH AND MEAT

The main problem here was that, apart from chicken portions, no meat or fish in the supermarket seemed to be packed in individual amounts. The smallest pack would feed two. I was a bit miffed about this because I ended up with more mince than I really wanted and so couldn't afford more variety. Mince, sausages and smoked herring are not the most interesting of meats or fish. Lucky I could afford the chicken breast . . .

Later I went back to the supermarket to have a chat with the butcher-in-charge. He told me that yes, you *can* have one chop or a few ounces of mince if that's all you want. Just ask and ye shall be given.

☆ *Choose meats that are priced at no more than £1 per pound (there is plenty of choice) and you need never spend more than £2 a week on section 1.*

Fish

Not all supermarkets have a fresh fish counter so it wasn't until a later week that I was able to find fresh fish that wasn't in a packet. Even so I plumped for the fish bits

MEAT AND FISH

Week 1

Supermarket packs.
Full prices paid
Total weight bought: 36oz
Allowance: £3.75p

14oz minced beef	87p
7oz chicken breast	75p
8oz pork/beef sausages	49p
7oz pack smoked herrings	44p
	Total: £2.55p
	Saved: £1.20p

Week 2

Supermarket packs. Special offers bought
Total weight bought: 35¾oz
Allowance: £3.75p

15oz minced beef 'special low price'	81p
5½oz chicken breast	66p
8oz pork sausages	56p
7¾oz pack smoked herring	48p
	Total: £2.51p

Money off stickers:
10p (sausages)   Actual Cost: £2.21p
20p (herrings)   Saved: £1.54p

Week 3

Local butcher/Supermarket fresh fish counter
Total weight bought: 44oz
Allowance: £3.75p

8oz sausages	44p
8oz minced beef	50p
4oz pigs liver	12p
8oz shin beef	72p
1lb fish bits	50p

Total: £2.28p
Saved: £1.47p

Week 4

From local butcher and supermarkets
Total weight bought: 30½oz
Allowance: £3.75p

7oz chicken breast	75p
7½oz smoked mackerel	45p
8oz fish bits	25p
8oz minced beef	50p

Total: £1.95p
Saved: £1.80p

(chunky pieces) because they are incredibly good value. Why pay more if you don't have to? What we often forget is that many really good fish dishes use assorted flaked fish, e.g. Old smokey soup and Kedgeree (opposite) and Fish pie (p.30). With some fish – like cod and haddock – being extremely expensive when sold in whole fillets or steaks, fish 'bits' are the ideal way to buy and perfect for the job.

It's good to have a treat now and then, though, and expensive prawns in their shells can be worth buying for a special occasion if you keep the bits you normally throw away. Use these to make a flavoursome stock:

Prawn stock

1 dessertspoon sunflower oil
½ carrot, diced (or carrot trimmings)
1 dessertspoon onion, chopped
Prawn shells, crushed
10fl oz (300ml) water

Heat the oil and gently fry the vegetables. Add the prawn shells and water. Cook gently for about 15 minutes until the liquid has reduced by a third. Strain through a sieve pressing down hard with a wooden spoon to extract maximum flavour. Cool and use to flavour soups, sauces, rice for Kedgeree, etc. Freeze if not being used within 24 hours.

☆ *Fish – because it is high in polyunsaturated fats – is better for you than red meat.*

Here are three good ways of stretching fish which is something I also find to be invaluable when entertaining (see pp. 114–115). It's incredible how something so inexpensive can make such good tasty meals and spreads.

Old smokey soup

Strictly speaking this soup should be made with smoked haddock although I've had good results using chunky white fish pieces together with smoked mackerel.

---

1 dessertspoon dried milk powder
5fl oz (150ml) water
2–3oz (50–75g) smoked fish, preferably haddock
Pepper to taste
1/2oz (15g) butter
1 dessertspoon onion, finely chopped
2oz (50g) potato, diced
1oz (25g) carrot, diced
1 dessertspoon celery, finely chopped
1 teaspoon flour

Blend the milk powder with the water. Put the fish in a shallow pan and pour in the 'milk'. Season with pepper. Bring to a simmer and cook for 5 minutes. Leave to stand for 5 minutes. Remove the fish and flake it. Keep the liquid on one side.

Melt the butter in a pan and add the vegetables. Cook over a low heat for 5 minutes. Stir in the flour and gradually add the fish liquid, stirring until thickened. Simmer for 10 minutes, then add the flaked fish and cook for a further 5 minutes.

Serve hot garnished with chopped fresh parsley if you have some on your windowsill (see Chapter 6).

Kedgeree

This recipe is an almost instant version of an old favourite using cooked rice and smoked herring. It's always worth cooking extra rice to use in a dish such as this.

Traditionally Kedgeree is seasoned with curry powder. I used a little mustard powder and dried ginger.

¹/₂oz (15g) butter
¹/₄ teaspoon dried ginger
¹/₄ teaspoon mustard powder
2 teaspoons sunflower oil
4oz (125g) cooked rice
4oz (125g) smoked herring, flaked
1 hardboiled egg, roughly chopped

Melt the butter in a pan over a moderate heat. Stir in the ginger and mustard. Cook for one minute. Add the oil. Stir in the rice and flaked fish and cook over a gentle heat until they are heated through. Fold in the egg and serve on a heated plate.

Flaked fish soufflé

If you have any spare egg yolk left from other recipes (see p.96) add it to the one specified here for a richer soufflé.

3oz (75g) chunky fish pieces
¹/₂oz (15g) butter
1 teaspoon lemon juice
¹/₂ teaspoon dried mustard
5fl oz (150ml) Basic white sauce (p.18)
Pepper
1 egg, separated
1 slice bread, crumbed
2 tablespoons Cheddar cheese, finely grated

Steam the fish over boiling water for 4–5 minutes until opaque. Remove skin and bones and flake the flesh.

Pre-heat the oven to gas mark 4, 350°F (180°C). Mix the lemon juice and mustard together and fold them into the hot white sauce. Season with pepper to taste. Beat in the egg yolk (or yolks) until the mixture is shiny and smooth. Fold in the fish and half the breadcrumbs.

Beat the egg white until stiff and fold into the soufflé mixture. Pour the mixture into a small pre-greased 1 pint soufflé dish. Mix the remaining crumbs with the cheese and sprinkle over the top. Bake for 30 minutes or until risen and golden.

Meat
Which chicken portion to buy? That was the question when choosing my meat. Had it been mid-winter I might have settled for the cheaper thighs and used them in a casserole (see p.26). But the weather was warm and I'd already decided to fit in at least *one* luxury, so I settled on the breast. This turned out to be a really good choice as it led me to experiment to justify buying an expensive portion in the first place. It really does seem that one breast can easily feed not one but two . . . and, with a bit of magic, even more.

Stuffed breast of chicken
Carefully remove the chicken breast from the bone, then slice the flesh through horizontally but not quite completely. Open out the 'pocket' and bash the meat to thinness. Using one of the suggestions below, spread some stuffing on one half of the chicken and fold over the other half. This makes a sizable parcel. If you want to stretch it to two servings slice the breast completely through and use each half to make up a parcel.

Stuffing suggestions:
- Spread meat from one skinned sausage over all the breast. Sprinkle with chopped prunes and fold. Roast or steam.
- Lay a 1oz slice of Cheddar cheese on the breast and fold. Egg, crumb and fry.

To cook: This can be done in several ways according to which method is most fuel-saving on the day (see pp.77–83) or how you wish to present the final dish. You can:

41

- Cover with bacon slices and roast for 30 minutes in a hot oven.
- Wrap in a lettuce leaf and steam over boiling water for 30 minutes.
- Coat with egg and crumbs, then shallow-fry for 15 minutes, turning once.

Serving suggestions:
- If steaming, serve with steamed celery and carrot sticks.
- If roasting, serve with roast potato slices and braised carrots.
- If frying, serve with a crisp green salad.

Gingered chicken with apricots

This substantial recipe is ideal if you want to make one chicken breast do the work of two because you can cut off and keep back 1 or 2oz (25 or 50g) of raw chicken breast to use in a stir-fry dish the following day (see opposite). Serve with boiled rice.

5fl oz water
1 tablespoon dried milk
1/2 small onion, chopped into wedges
Pepper to taste
1 chicken breast
1 teaspoon dried ginger
1oz butter
4 dried apricots, soaked overnight
2 teaspoons plain flour
1 slice brown bread, crumbed

Put the water, dried milk, onion and pepper into a pan. Stir to dissolve the milk powder, then bring to the boil. Remove from the heat and leave to infuse.

Remove the chicken from the bone (use this to make stock). Dice the flesh and toss in the dried ginger. Melt the butter in a pan and lightly fry the chicken. Transfer to a greased casserole. Add the halved, drained apricots.

Stir the flour into the remaining juices in the pan (add the onion to the casserole) and cook for 1 minute. Gradually stir the milk into the roux until you have a thick sauce. Pour the sauce over the chicken and fold everything together gently. Scatter over the crumbs and bake in the oven at gas mark 4, 350°F (180°C) for 20 minutes.

Lemon chicken stir-fry

This is a lovely way to make the most of a few vegetables and an ounce or two of chicken breast. It's a hob-top dish that is speedy to cook.

Juice of one lemon
1 teaspoon cornflour
1 dessertspoon honey
1 dessertspoon soy sauce
1 tablespoon sunflower oil
2–3oz (50–75g) chicken breast, cut into thin strips
1/2 onion, cut into chunks
5fl oz (150ml) in volume of a mixture of shredded celery and matchstick carrots
1 teaspoon grated lemon rind
1 tablespoon peanuts
Black pepper to taste (preferably freshly ground)

Measure the lemon juice and add enough water to make up to 4fl oz (115ml). Blend in the cornflour, honey and soy sauce. Set aside.

Heat the oil in a pan and sauté the chicken and vegetables for about 5 minutes until the meat turns white. Stir in the lemon rind, the cornflour mixture and the peanuts. Bring to the boil over a medium heat, stirring until the sauce thickens and coats the meat and vegetables. Reduce the heat and simmer for 4 minutes. Season with pepper to taste.

Serve with hot Savoury rice (see p.32).

It wasn't until I got to the local butcher in the second week that I really began to enjoy myself in this section. In fact I got so carried away with the variety and the fact that this time I could buy exactly the amount I wanted that, even though I still didn't spend all my £3.75p, I ended up buying more than I really needed. The surplus had to be frozen away for a later week.

There are plenty of cheaper meats available from butchers. I could have had my pick from pork spare rib chops, belly pork, breast of lamb, bacon joints, stewing steak and several types of offal. Because of comparison costing and trying to avoid overly fatty meats I settled on the ever-useful best mince, liver and shin of beef, supplemented by the sausages. (There are some very good low-fat sausages on the market – stick to these for your health's sake.) Here are some of the dishes I made with my choices (see also pp.112–116).

Frikadeller

I use shin beef for this Danish dish which has a deal more 'body' than most bought mince.

2oz shin beef
2oz bacon
1/2 onion
1/2 slice brown bread
2 tablespoons beaten egg (see p.25)
Pepper
Butter or sunflower oil for frying

Mince together the meat, bacon and onion. Soak the bread in water, squeeze it nearly dry and mix it in with the meat. Stir in the egg and season to taste with pepper. Shape into ovals and shallow-fry for 10 minutes, on each side.

Variations: These are also tasty made with a mixture of minced beef and sausagemeat. (I de-skinned a sausage.)

44

For a change tuck a small piece of Cheddar cheese into the centre of each Frikadeller before frying.

Chilli con carne

Traditionally this is made with cubed steak and not with the everyday mince that I so often use, so there is no reason why minced shin beef could not be used instead. In a recipe such as this beef is beef as far as I'm concerned. And apologies to all those who think differently.

---

1 tablespoon sunflower oil
1/2 onion, chopped
4oz (125g) minced beef
1 dessertspoon chilli powder
Pinch mixed herbs
1/2 teaspoon ground ginger
1 tablespoon tomato purée
10fl oz (300ml) beef stock or water
Pepper
2oz (50g) cooked red kidney beans (at a pinch you could use baked beans)

Heat the oil in a pan and lightly fry the onion for a few minutes. Add the meat and cook gently, stirring until browned. Sprinkle over the chilli powder, herbs and ginger. Cook for five minutes, stirring regularly. Add the tomato purée, stock and pepper to taste, bring to the boil and cook for about 30 minutes until the meat is tender. Stir in the beans and cook for a further 5 minutes. Accompany with pitta bread (p.92) and salad.

☆ Always buy the best quality mince you can afford. Gristle and fat you don't need. The more actual meat the higher the protein content will be.

Glazed meat loaf

This is a good cut-and-come again meat loaf, sweet and succulent with the addition of apples, carrots and a honey glaze. Eat hot one day, the next day cold with salad. The remainder can be sliced thinly for sandwiches.

To make it go even further add just 1 more slice of bread (crumbed) and the other half of the egg.

---

1 crisp apple (about 4oz/125g), peeled, cored and grated
4oz (125g) minced beef
1 slice brown bread, crumbed
1/2 onion, grated
1 medium carrot, grated
1 dessertspoon brown sauce
1/2 egg (2 tablespoons), beaten
1 dessertspoon tomato purée
1 heaped teaspoon honey

Mix together the apple, beef, breadcrumbs, onion, carrot and brown sauce. Stir in the egg. Mix together thoroughly and press into a small (1lb) greased loaf tin. Blend together the tomato purée and honey and spread over the meat mixture. Cook at gas mark 3, 325°F (170°C) for 1 hour, then cover with foil, turn out the heat and leave in the oven for a further 15 minutes.

By the fourth week I was able to buy less meat than before (only 30oz) because by then I'd built up that stock of essential (cheaper) vegetable protein: lentils, pulses and oatmeal, which when cooked with the meat made it go a lot further. I could even cut out meat altogether and go vegetarian now and again. Things were looking good.

 Freeze mince the easy way. Put a few ounces in a polybag and roll out into thin flat sheets. When frozen these thaw very quickly and small bits can be snapped off if that's all you need – for the following soup, for example.

Mulligatawny Soup

I have hundreds of cookbooks yet only two contain a recipe for mulligatawny soup, and I find neither of them inspiring. So I've invented my own. When I demonstrated it on BBC TV's Bazaar programme it was sampled by the crew before the show and proved so popular that I had to make some more. The chutney and curry powder were not on my original shopping list, but are high on my list of 'extras' for the storecupboard.

---

1 dessertspoon sunflower oil
1–2oz (25–50g) minced beef
1 small apple, peeled, cored and sliced
1 teaspoon curry powder
1/2 teaspoon flour
1 teaspoon tomato purée
1 teaspoon mango chutney
10fl oz (300ml) beef stock
1 teaspoon long-grain rice

Heat the oil in a pan and fry the beef. Add the sliced apple and cook for 5 minutes. Stir in the curry powder and flour and cook for a further minute. Stir in the tomato purée, the chutney and the stock until well blended. For a really smooth soup liquidise at this point.

Bring to the boil and simmer for 15 minutes.* Stir in the rice and cook for a further 20 minutes, adding a little more stock or water if the soup becomes too thick. Serve hot with crusty bread.

*   If you wish to make the soup in bulk, cook to this point, then freeze. After thawing add the rice and continue as directed.

DAIRY PRODUCE

Eggs, milk and cheese are an excellent and cheaper source of animal protein than meat or fish – something to bear in mind when you come to this section of your shopping. In fact Cheddar cheese – ounce for ounce – has more protein than steak. But it also contains fat. Every silver lining has a cloud.

Milk

A lot depends upon life-style as to how much milk a person needs to buy during a week. Although half-a-pint-per-person-per-day is the usual intake, some of this might be drunk away from home, for instance in coffee at work. On the other hand your own supply could be drunk by someone else – like the gas-man. And what about those six friends who suddenly decided to drop in for tea? For times like this it's useful to have a back-up supply such as dried milk or a carton of long-life.

☆ *Mix together equal quantities of reconstituted dried milk and fresh milk. The flavour of dried milk is then undetectable.*

☆ *Stir a little skimmed dried milk into fresh skimmed milk to give a richer flavour without the added fat.*

Now although I normally buy all my milk over the doorstep and still continue to do so, during the four weeks of 'The Challenge' I bought my milk solely from the supermarket. This was because the long-life skimmed milk in cartons was the cheapest way to buy all my milk in one go. Sometimes it pays to be unfaithful. But I missed my milkman and I don't recommend the practice. (Sorry Gerald, I promise not to do it again.)

☆ *Skimmed milk is marginally higher in protein than full cream and generally lower in price.*

48

Once I had bought some dried milk (week 2) I was able to cut down the amount of fresh by a pint and still have enough to make my own yogurt. Lately I've had a preference for the thick-set yogurt which substitutes beautifully for whipped cream and can always be thinned down with a little milk if needed.

Thick-set yoghurt

1 teaspoon cornflour
10fl oz (300ml) milk
1 dessertspoon dried milk
1 dessertspoon thick yogurt

Blend the cornflour with a little of the milk. Stir into the rest of the milk together with the dried milk and bring to the boil. Simmer for 3 minutes and then cool to blood heat. Stir in the thick yogurt, cover and leave to set in a very warm place for 8 hours. Drain off any water that rises to the top, then store the yogurt in the fridge.

Sweet yogurt dressing
This is gorgeous served with fresh and dried fruit salads (p.119), fruit pies, babas (p.90) or wherever you would use cream as a dessert dressing.

1 heaped dessertspoon thick yogurt (see above)
1 teaspoon honey
1 teaspoon grated lemon rind
1 dessertspoon orange juice
A squeeze of lemon juice

Blend all the ingredients together.

 The juice of a lemon is usually too much for a one-person portion. Instead just stick in a fork, twist slightly and squeeze out the few drops you'll need.

DAIRY PRODUCE

Week I

All from supermarket . Full prices paid
Allowance: £3.75p

2 litres long-life skimmed milk	70p
I pint long-life skimmed milk	20p
6 eggs (grade 3)	48p
250g concentrated butter	31p
500g table margarine	29p
I Ioz Cheddar cheese	72p
I 5oz tub thick-set yogurt	49p

Total: £3.19p
Saved: 56p

Week 2

All from supermarket (special offers sought)
Allowance: £3.75p

2 litres long-life skimmed milk	70p
6 eggs (grade 3)	42p
9 oz Cheddar cheese	59p
3 × 5oz tubs thick-set yogurt	48p

Total: £2.19p

Eggs down in price.
Yogurt I p cheaper if bought
in smaller tubs   Saved: £1.56p

Week 3

Local shops.
Allowance: £3.75p

2 litres long-life skimmed milk	70p
6 eggs (grade 2)	40p
250g concentrated butter	31p
500g table margarine	29p
9oz Cheddar cheese	59p
	Total: £2.29p

All from supermarkets except eggs,
which were cheaper and *larger* from
butcher. (Made my own yogurt this week.) Saved: £1.46p

Week 4

'Hotch-potch'
Allowance: £3.75p

2 litres long-life skimmed milk	70p
6 eggs (grade 2)	40p
9 oz Cheddar cheese	59p
	Total: £1.69p

Milk and cheese from supermarket.
Eggs from butcher.
Yogurt – homemade.

Saved: £2.06p

Cheese

The flavour of cheese is always more pronounced when eaten at room temperature. Nevertheless I find if I use my Cheddar straight from the fridge it makes it easier to grate. Grated cheese seems to go on for ever – one of the reasons why I bought less after week 1.

I made my own 'spreading' cheese by draining about 8fl oz (250ml) yogurt overnight in a muslin bag suspended over a bowl. This produces several ounces of an admirable substitute for soft curd cheese.

☆ *For imitation Parmesan harden cheese by leaving a few ounces in the fridge unwrapped. Use the finest grater for best results.*

☆ *Keep boxes of grated cheese ready in the freezer for instant use.*

☆ *Fresh brown breadcrumbs and grated cheese make a good savoury topping instead of mashed potato. Mix together and bake or grill until golden and crusty.*

Glamorgan sausages

This is a traditional British dish made with cheese which just goes to show that our ancestors knew all about economising. Serve with a crisp green salad and keep your meat for another day.

1oz (25g) Cheddar cheese, grated
1oz (25g) fresh brown breadcrumbs
1 dessertspoon grated onion
¼ teaspoon dry mustard
Pepper to taste
1 egg, separated
2 teaspoons water
2 dessertspoons sunflower oil

In a bowl mix together the cheese, half the breadcrumbs, the onion, mustard and pepper. Blend the egg yolk with the water and stir into the mixture until it binds to a compact ball. If too dry add more water a drop at a time.

Divide the mixture into two portions and roll each into a sausage shape. Dip into the egg white and then into the remaining crumbs. Heat the oil in a small pan over a high heat and fry the 'sausages', turning them so that they cook and brown evenly.

Fats

They say that eating butter is not good for you but I really don't think you can beat that luxury flavour – just now and again. Concentrated butter is very cheap and goes much further than you would think so it's perfect for penny-pinchers. Although it's intended for cooking I found that a smidgin worked into table margarine made a very edible spreadable.

If you buy full cream doorstep milk and you have a liquidiser then it's perfectly possible to turn dairy-maid and make a few ounces of your very own butter, just enough for one person. Collect the cream from the milk over several days (it keeps quite well in the fridge) until you have about 10fl oz (300ml), then follow these directions.

Home-made butter

Put the cream in the liquidiser and blend at medium speed for about 1 minute. The cream will first thicken and then begin to separate.

Add 2 tablespoons of cold water and continue blending for a further 30 seconds. Drain through a sieve, reserving the liquid (see following tip).

Return the butter to the liquidiser and add a further ½ tea-cup of cold water. Whizz until the butter forms large lumps. Drain again and 'work' the butter on a plate using a knife or spatula to remove the excess water. Form into a block – this should make 3–4oz (75–125g) according to the time of year (i.e. richness of the cream) – and wrap in greaseproof paper. Store in the fridge.

☆ *The drained liquid from the first stage of butter-making described above is buttermilk. This is excellent for scone- and bread-making. Alternatively turn the buttermilk back into 'skimmed milk' by stirring in some dried milk.*

Margarine is not strictly 'dairy' but I know you won't mind if I lump it in with the rest. It sort of fits in better with this section. There is a wide range of margarine so I picked a middle-of-the-road brand. Once I'd got my budget under control I knew I would be able to change to buying the low-cholesterol brands which are more expensive but better for me.

Here's a way of making a cheap hard margarine go further and end up lower in calories. The oil helps to make it spread more easily when chilled, though originally I made it without.

Easy-spread margarine

8oz (250g) hard margarine
3–4fl oz (75–115ml) warm water
1–2 teaspoons sunflower oil (optional)

Cut margarine into small cubes, then *slowly* beat in the warm water until the mixture becomes soft and fluffy. Beat in the oil (remember though that it adds calories and pennies).

Pack the margarine into tubs and store in the fridge. Use at room temperature for spreading. *Don't* use for frying.

Speaking of oil, I always buy polyunsaturated sunflower oil nowadays. It may be more expensive than the type labelled simply 'cooking oil' but I'm convinced it's better for my health.

If you have to grease a frying-pan do it the economical way. Dip kitchen paper into oil and wipe round the pan instead of pouring in oil.

FRUIT AND VEGETABLES

This section probably more than any other was where I really felt the pinch, especially as I couldn't afford to buy much fresh fruit – normally I eat a lot.

Obviously the thing to do is to look at prices first and then decide which is the best buy. For instance I bought the more expensive iceberg lettuce as it was a good size and would last a long time. Because it was crisp I could also braise it and so use it as a cooked vegetable.

Not every vegetable is priced by weight. Every time things are priced by the pack I always check the weights to make sure I get value for money. Those few 'free' ounces extra mean I can buy less of something else. So pick out the heaviest head of celery from a pile being sold at one price and you could be on to a winner. But then again, I could have got there first.

The most important thing to remember is that all fruits and vegetables have their own season and at least once a year will be at their cheapest (fortunately not all at the same time so you get endless variety). Many are available all the year round – don't take these for granted and do take note of the price.

Don't ever feel obliged to buy set weights just because they are priced in that way. When one courgette is just enough for one person why ask for half a pound? Only buy the amount that *you* feel you need. If there are sulks – shop elsewhere.

Nevertheless, with a vegetable like cabbage it can be hard to buy a small amount. If you end up buying and cooking too much *don't* throw it away. Use it for the following recipe.

Rumbledethumps

This is a lovely Scottish dish which is based on equal
quantities of potato and cabbage. Because it can be made
with leftovers, why not use potato saved from its skin
(p.29)?

Equal quantities of cooked potato and cooked cabbage, the
amount depending on your appetite
1 dessertspoon grated onion
1 teaspoon butter
Grated Cheddar cheese
Pepper

Mash the potatoes with the butter, season with pepper
and fold in the chopped cabbage and grated onion. Put
into an ovenproof dish and sprinkle over some grated
cheese. Heat in the oven on gas mark 5, 375°F (190°C) for
about 15 minutes until the cheese is bubbling. For extra
flavour fold in chopped crisply fried bacon.

Fruit

Recently I went into a greengrocers and was just about to
break into a bunch of three bananas (because I only
wanted two) when I was stopped by the shop-keeper. He
gave me two bananas from a larger bunch with the excuse
that when he was left with one banana no-one would buy
it. Have you noticed how bananas always come in two or
threes and never singly? Are we being pressured to buy
more than we need? Worth thinking about. It's a little
things like that that take the money.

☆ *Soak a whole unpeeled banana in cold water for at least*
10 minutes before peeling and slicing. This prevents it
going brown too quickly on contact with air.

Chart showing the most popular vegetables
and the months when they are likely to be at their
cheapest. Allow for adverse weather conditions holding
back crops.

	Jan	Feb	Mar	Apr	May	Jun	Jul	Aug	Sept	Oct	Nov	Dec
Beetroot										■		
Broad beans						■	■					
Broccoli	■	■									■	■
Brussels sprouts	■	■	■									
Carrots	■											
Cauliflower									■	■		
Celery								■	■			
Chinese leaves			■									
Courgettes								■	■	■		
Leeks	■	■		■							■	
Lettuce						■	■					
Marrow								■				
Parsnips	■	■									■	
Peas						■	■					
Red cabbage			■								■	
Runner beans								■	■			
Spinach					■							
Spring greens				■	■							
Swedes	■											
Sweetcorn										■		
Tomatoes									■	■		
White cabbage									■	■	■	■

FRUIT AND VEGETABLES

Week I

All from supermarket.
Allowance: £3.75p

8oz (5 small) tomatoes	23p
I iceberg lettuce (I ½lb)	70p
Head of celery (I ½lb)	78p
I pack (2½lb) apples	76p
I2oz carrots	22p
I2oz onions	12p
2lb potatoes	40p
2 bananas (small)	10p
I lemon	10p
Total:	£3.41p
Saved:	34p

Week 2

All from supermarket (special offers sought out)
Allowance: £3.75p

8oz tomatoes (4)	23p
I crisp lettuce	59p
2lb apples (loose)	76p
I2oz carrots	22p
8oz onions	8p
2 bananas	12p
2 lemons	20p
I cabbage (firm hearted)	38p
	£2.58p
Less 30p money-off sticker on cabbage	30p
Total:	£2.28p
Saved:	£1.47p

Week 3

All except tomatoes from local green grocer.
Tomatoes from butcher (cheapest place).
Allowance: £3.75p

1 Chinese leaves (2¾lb)	60p
½ cucumber	10p
2lb potatoes	32p
2lb apples (loose)	70p
8oz onions	8p
1 flat lettuce	20p
8oz tomatoes (4)	20p
8oz carrots	12p

Total: £2.32p
Saved: £1.43p

Week 4

Various shops
Allowance: £3.75p

1 crisp lettuce	56p
2lbs apples (loose)	70p
Head of celery	56p
12oz onions	12p
8oz carrots	12p
2 bananas	15p
1 lemon	15p
8oz tomatoes (5)	20p

Total: £2.62p
Saved: £1.13p

☆ *Half a banana will keep quite well for 24 hours if you peel down only to the amount you need. Remove this and then, leaving the remainder unpeeled, fold back a bit of loose skin over the exposed end. Wrap tightly in cling film. Only the cut surface will discolour and when you cut this off the rest will be perfect.*

There is nothing to beat the flavour of real lemon and one can go quite a long way if you follow one or two tips:

☆ *Freeze surplus lemon juice in ice-cube trays. Remember to label once frozen as it's easily mistaken for stock or egg-white.*

☆ *Buy a new nail brush and keep this especially for when you are grating lemon zest. Use it to brush down the grater and collect all the bits of zest that are normally impossible to move. Then, working from the furthest end of the brush and always towards you (otherwise you get a face full), draw a knife across the bristles and the zest flicks out. Finally tap the brush face down on a plate. This way you get twice as much zest as you normally would.*

☆ *Whole lemons that have had their zest grated off quickly turn mouldy. Prevent this by wrapping tightly in cling-film and keeping in the fridge. Soak used lemon shells in water for several hours. Then strain the liquid and use it as a hair rinse or for cooking rice (see p.32).*

Apples are not just useful as a between-meals snack or in desserts as this savoury flan demonstrates.

Onion and Apple Flan
This is a good filling for an individual quiche (see p.96). Remember that as you only need part of the specified egg and milk mixture for this small serving you can use the rest to make something else (see p.94).

Shortcrust pastry
½ small onion, sliced into thin rings
1 crisp apple, peeled and cored
Pinch mixed herbs
Pepper
3fl oz (75ml) egg/milk mixture
(proportions: 2 eggs to ¼ pint milk)

Line a small greased flan tin with shortcrust pastry and cover with a layer of onion. Top with thinly sliced apple. Repeat layers until the tin is full.

Stir the herbs and pepper into the egg and milk mixture and pour over the onions and apple. Bake at gas mark 4–5, 350–375°F (180–190°C) for 30 minutes.

Variation:
Try onion with lightly fried bacon or onion with cheese.

Apple bread pudding
This is quite a substantial pudding – almost a meal in itself, which is not bad for a dessert. So if you fancy something sweet, try this.

---

1 apple, peeled, cored and chopped
1 slice wholewheat bread, cut into cubes
1 dessertspoon sultanas
½ oz (15g) butter, melted
1 egg
4fl oz (115ml) milk
1 dessertspoon sugar

Mix together the apple, bread and sultanas in a bowl. Drizzle over the melted butter and mix well.

Beat the egg with the milk and sugar and fold into the apple mixture. Spoon into a greased pie dish. Stand this in a larger container containing hot water to a depth of 1 inch (2.5cm). Bake in the oven at gas mark 4, 350°F (180°C) for 30–40 minutes or until the centre is cooked through.

61

Honey baked bananas

A good pud to make when you've the oven on for something else. Alternatively cook it on the hob in a covered frying-pan.

---

1 firm banana
1 dessertspoon butter (melted)
1 dessertspoon honey
1 dessertspoon orange juice
1 dessertspoon walnuts, finely chopped

Peel the banana and cut it in half. Split each half lengthways to make four pieces in all. Place in a shallow dish and brush with melted butter.

Blend together the honey and orange juice and spoon this over the bananas. Sprinkle with the nuts.

Bake in a pre-heated oven at gas mark 5, 375°F (190°C) for 7–10 minutes. Serve hot.

Note: If you haven't any walnuts sprinkle over breadcrumbs fried in butter and tossed with a pinch of dried ginger.

Variation:
For a special occasion substitute rum for orange juice.

Vegetables

Several vegetables lasted me longer than seven days so I could buy less the next time I went shopping. Celery in particular can last up to three weeks and goes an especially long way when shredded. Store it in the fridge loosely wrapped in polythene.

With its pronounced flavour celery can be used in quite small amounts and is an excellent substitute for salt in cooking. I always look for sticks that have plenty of young green leaf shoots because these are good to add to salads.

☆ *While not overly high in vitamin and mineral content,
celery is reputedly one of the best vegetables to eat if you
suffer from rheumatism.*

Braised celery au gratin

This celery dish can be prepared in advance and popped
into the oven along with other things. View it either as a
vegetable to go with your main dish or as a vegetable lunch
dish in its own right.

4oz (125g) celery, cut into chunks
1 dessertspoon onion, chopped
Sunflower oil
Pepper
1 heaped tablespoon thick-set yogurt (see p.49)
1 tablespoon chicken or beef stock
Pinch mixed herbs
1oz (25g) butter, melted
1 slice bread, crumbed
1/2oz (15g) Cheddar cheese, grated

Lightly fry the celery and onion in a little oil for 2–3
minutes, then transfer to a well greased ovenproof dish.
Season with pepper to taste. Mix together the yogurt,
stock and herbs and spoon over the vegetables. Mix
together the melted butter, breadcrumbs and cheese and
scatter this over the vegetables and sauce. Bake in the
oven on gas mark 4 or 5, 350–375°F (180–190°C) for
about 25 minutes until the top is crisp and golden.
As an alternative to vegetables 'in the piece', try serving
them as a purée. Once cooked and tender, mash, sieve or
process the well drained vegetables to a smooth paste.
Add a smidgin of butter and re-heat to serve. For a very
satisfying mid-day snack fill a potato shell with hot
vegetable purée and top with a poached egg.

Vegetarian lasagne

This is a good example of a recipe that uses ingredients already prepared or cooked – the type of recipe you can *plan* for. For instance, you could make the Lentil croquette recipe on p.70 and cook extra lentils for this dish at the same time. The cooked vegetables could be yesterday's planned left-overs and the Tomato sauce (p.92) and grated cheese would be ready and waiting in the fridge/freezer.

2oz (50g) lasagne (see pp.70–71)
½ onion, chopped
1 dessertspoon oil
4oz cooked whole lentils (green or brown)
2 tablespoons Tomato sauce (p.92)
½ teaspoon mixed herbs
4oz (125g) cooked mixed vegetables, e.g. carrots, celery, cabbage, courgette etc.
2oz (50g) grated cheese

Put the lasagne in a large pan of boiling water and cook until tender (see tips below). Fry the onion gently in the oil and, when golden, stir in the lentils and tomato sauce. Add the herbs and, lastly, the chopped vegetables. Cook for 2–3 minutes until well heated through. Lay one-third of the lasagne in a small greased dish and top with half the vegetable mixture. Repeat and then finish with another layer of lasagne. Tuck in the edges and cover with grated cheese. Pop under a pre-heated grill for 10 minutes until the cheese is bubbling.

☆ *To cook long pieces of lasagne use a meat tin half filled with water on top of the stove instead of a saucepan. Place the pasta strips in the bubbling water one at a time to avoid them sticking together. Once cooked, drain and sprinkle with a little oil.*

☆ For small portions and dishes I break the long pieces of lasagna in half crosswise – this makes it easier to handle and cook.

Spicy cabbage with apple . . . plus

This is a dual dish. First you have the spicy cabbage as an accompanying vegetable to the meat of the day, secondly the planned leftovers are cooked in chicken broth to make *soupe du jour* for the next day. The quantities given make 2 side vegetable servings or 1 side vegetable and 1 soup serving.

2oz (50g) bacon, diced
2 teaspoons sunflower oil
1 small onion, finely sliced
6oz (175g) red or green cabbage, finely shredded
1 medium apple, peeled, cored and sliced
$1/2$ teaspoon ground ginger
Pepper

Fry the bacon in the oil until crisp. Remove with a slotted spoon and put aside. Add the onion, cabbage and apple to the pan and lightly fry until the apple is tender. Sprinkle over the ginger and pepper to taste. Stir well and fry until the cabbage is cooked but still has 'bite'.

Serve half the vegetables, garnished with half the crispy bacon, to accompany your main meal. Transfer the rest to a covered dish and store in the fridge along with the remaining bacon. Next day stir the cooked vegetables into 5fl oz (150ml) chicken stock and simmer, covered, for 20 minutes until the cabbage is very soft. Blend in a liquidiser and serve piping hot with the remaining crispy bacon sprinkled on top.

There's an awful lot more to vegetables than first meets the eye as I was later to discover in my quest for Knowledge. So read up on Chapter 6 before spending your money – you could be in for a surprise . . .

GROCERIES

The allowance of £3.75 proved to be too little when it came to buying the groceries, but because I had managed to save on the other three sections there was enough money to buy what I needed. By the end of each week there was always money left over – admittedly only coppers at first but steadily it got better and by the end of the four weeks there was cash in hand to the value of £9.95 and *loads* left in the storecupboard.

Not many essential things needed replacing each week so up to a point I could have coped on the £3.75p as long as I was prepared to go without additional 'keeping' foods. I would have been perfectly healthy but terribly bored. There's nothing like having a few bits and bobs around to play with to make you feel like a proper cook.
Here is an example of how quite ordinary storecupboard ingredients can turn into something that you might normally have expected to buy:

Salad cream

1/2 level teaspoon dry mustard
Pepper to taste
3fl oz (75ml) evaporated milk
2fl oz (50ml) sunflower oil
2 dessertspoons vinegar
1 teaspoon sugar

Put the mustard and pepper into a bowl. Add the evaporated milk and mix well. Slowly beat in the oil. Add the vinegar and sugar and continue beating. The mixture will thicken. Store in a screw-top jar in the fridge.

☆ *Instead of buying packs of individual dried fruits buy one pack of mixed dried fruit salad. Use the prunes, apricots and peaches for cooking, and chop the pear and apple rings for nibbles – far better for you than sweeties.*

Pulses are excellent storecupboard food and full of

protein. The following two recipes are made with lentils which don't take quite as long to cook as the other types.

Cooking lentils

Unlike other pulses, lentils don't need a pre-soak. Just put them in a pan with about 1 inch (2.5cm) of water above them. Bring to the boil, then simmer until they are soft. This takes from 10 minutes for red split lentils to 30 minutes for whole green lentils. Also, the longer they have been in storage the longer they take to cook. Start checking after 10 minutes and add more boiling water if necessary.

 For a speedy short-cut to an overnight soak add 1 lb (500g) dried pulses to 2 1/2 pints (1.4 litre) of hot water and boil for 4 minutes. Cover and leave to stand for 1 hour, then strain and cover with plenty of fresh water. Boil rapidly again for 10 minutes, then simmer until tender.

Lentil and tomato soup

This is a really·thick nourishing soup good for those cold wintry days. For a lighter summer soup just omit the lentils. Ring the changes by using beef stock instead of chicken and adding a dash of brown sauce for extra 'bite'.

7oz (200g) tinned tomatoes
1 dessertspoon tomato purée
1/2 teaspoon sugar
5fl oz (150ml) chicken stock
1oz (25g) red split lentils
Pepper to taste

Mash or liquidise the tomatoes and rub through a sieve to remove the seeds. Put the tomato pulp into a saucepan and blend in the tomato purée. Add the sugar, chicken stock and lentils. Bring to the boil and simmer until the lentils are soft (about 15 minutes). Season with plenty of pepper and serve hot with a sprinkling of grated cheese. *Note:* For a creamier consistency whizz the soup in a liquidiser and then re-heat.

GROCERIES

Week 1

All from supermarket
Allowance: £3.75p
plus £2.10p saved from other
sections = £5.85p

Cereal 350g	75p
1 carton orange juice	43p
1 large sliced brown loaf	44p
1 pkt tea leaves	37p
1 50g jar instant coffee	53p
1 tin tomatoes	14p
1 tin tomato puree	17p
1 tub baking powder	29p
0·5 litre sunflower oil	52p
1 bottle vinegar	20p
1 pkt jelly	16p
1 small tin evaporated milk	21p
1·5kg flour (plain white)	43p
1kg granulated sugar	44p
1 pkt cream crackers	17p
1 tub pepper	29p
1 tin baked beans	23p

Total: £5.78p
Saved: 7p overall

Week 2

All from supermarket
Allowance: £3.75p plus £4.57p
from savings = £8.32p

1 carton orange juice	4⁚
1 large sliced brown loaf	4⁚
1 pack bacon pieces	79
1 tin tomatoes	1⁚
1 tin baked beans	2⁚
1 pack dried milk (makes 5 pints)	5⁚
1lb long-grain rice	4⁚
1lb lentils	59
375g sultanas	59
500g porridge oats	3⁚
1 tub mixed dried herbs	2⁚
1 small tin mustard	3⁚
1 tub chilli powder	2⁚
1 bottle brown sauce	3⁚

Total: £5.6⁚
Saved: £2.66p over

Week 3

All from supermarket
Allowance: £3.75p plus £4.36p
from savings = £8.11p

Cereal 500g	56p
1 large sliced brown loaf	43p
1 50g jar instant coffee	53p
1 litre rapeseed oil	69p
1 pkt cream crackers	17p
1 tin tomatoes	14p
1 tin tomato puree	19p
1 tin sardines	24p
1 lb dried red kidney beans	76p
1 lb jar honey	82p
1 pkt jelly	16p
1 tin evaporated milk	21p
1 tub ground ginger	20p
1 carton orange juice	43p

Total: £5.50p
Saved: £2.61p overall

Week 4

All from supermarket
Allowance: £3.75p plus £4.99p
from savings = £8.74p

1 large brown loaf	44p
1 tin tomatoes	14p
1·5kg wholewheat flour	53p
1 carton orange juice	43p
1 lb mung bean seeds	55p
250g mixed dried fruit salad	76p
1 bottle soy sauce	35p
500g wholewheat spaghetti	48p
1 pkt (5 sachets) gelatine	45p

Total: £4.13p
Saved: £4.61p overall

Lentil croquettes

1 canned tomato, drained and chopped
1oz (25g) Cheddar cheese, grated
4oz (125g) brown breadcrumbs
½ beaten egg
Pinch dry mustard
Pepper
3oz (75g) cooked whole lentils (see pp.64 and 67)
Flour, preferably wholewheat
Sunflower oil

Mix all the ingredients together except the lentils, flour and oil. Then stir in the lentils. Form the mixture into 4 rounds and coat with flour. Shallow-fry for a few minutes on each side in hot oil until golden.

Variation: Omit the cheese and add a pinch of mixed herbs.

As long as you get in a store of the basic food items you can always be sure of making something interesting. For example, you'll have noticed that I didn't buy pasta until the fourth week. Yet I was able to eat it from the beginning. This was because I had the makings right from the start. All I had to do was throw them together, mess them around a bit and then 'Presto! Pasta!'

Basic pasta dough

4oz (125g) plain flour
1 egg
1 dessertspoon sunflower oil

Put the flour in a basin and add the egg and oil. Mix together with a fork until the mixture binds together. Add a drop or two of water if the mixture is too dry.

Knead the dough very well for at least five minutes, then wrap in greaseproof paper and leave to stand at room temperature for about an hour. Roll the dough out *very* thinly and cut into thin strips (tagliatelle), wide strips (lasagne) or leave in sheets and make ravioli (p.115). Dust the pasta lightly with flour to prevent it from sticking together. (Pasta can be prepared in advance and kept in a flour-dusted polythene bag for up to 24 hours.)

Cook in plenty of fast-boiling water to which a dessertspoon of oil has been added. After about 5 minutes, test and taste. The pasta should be 'al dente': just tender but still with a 'bite' to it.

Pasta alla carbonara

Make up the basic pasta recipe above and roll out very thinly. Cut into narrow ribbons. Dust with flour and leave for half an hour to dry out slightly.

When you are ready to cook, bring a large saucepan ¾ full of water to the boil. Sprinkle in 1 dessertspoon cooking oil (this prevents the pasta sticking together) and drop in the pasta ribbons. Stir gently to be sure they are not sticking, then cook over a high heat for about 5 minutes until tender.

Meanwhile fry 4oz (125g) finely chopped bacon in a little butter until crisp and, off the heat, stir in 2 tablespoons plain yogurt. When the pasta is cooked, drain thoroughly in a colander, sprinkle over a little sunflower oil and toss. Add to the bacon and yogurt mixture, mix well, then stir in 1 beaten egg and 2oz (50g) finely grated cheese – the heat from the pasta will cook the egg. Eat at once.

 Remember that home-made pasta cooks in half the time of the bought variety.

Grocery extras

The grocery items I bought in the four weeks of 'The Challenge' were what I consider to be essentials. This is a list of 'secondaries' which I would have gone on to buy to build up my storecupboard.

Assorted flours:
Start with wholewheat flour (you can now buy a
self-raising variety) and strong plain flour. With these you
then have a choice of making wholewheat pasta, pastry
and pancakes, not to mention brown and white breads
and buns.

Cornflour:
Useful not just for custards and sauces and general
thickening, but also to include in cakes and biscuits for a
closer texture than ordinary flour gives.

Semolina:
Use for puddings and gnocchi (p.111) and in cakes (p.108).

Sugars:
If you have a liquidiser you can grind granulated sugar
down to caster and, with a coffee grinder, go on to make
fine icing sugar. But with your savings you can afford to buy
caster and icing sugar for those special recipes. Grind
down demerara sugar to make 'soft brown'.

Muscovado sugar:
This has a very rich treacly flavour which is good in
gingerbreads, biscuits and crumbles.

Syrup and treacle:
Worth having for parkins, puddings and tarts.

Raising agents:
Bicarbonate of soda and 'instant' (vitamin C-added) yeast.
Generally used for baking, 'bicarb' is also good for mixing
with a little water to wash down the insides of ovens and
refrigerators.
  'Instant' yeast is just that. No need to do anything more
than mix with flour following the directions on the packet.
As speedy as using a bread mix.

Dried pulses and grains:
There's such a wide variety from which to choose, my
favourites being whole green lentils (they have quite a

different flavour from that of the red split ones); butter beans; split peas; chick peas; pearl barley.

Tip: Look for 'pot' barley which is unpolished pearl barley. It has a higher nutritional content.

Nuts:
Peanuts, flaked almonds and walnuts all add crunch and flavour to sweet and savoury dishes.

Tip: Prolong the shelf life of shelled nuts by storing them in the freezer.

Sauces and condiments:
Worcestershire and Tabasco sauces add that extra 'bite' to a dish. Mango chutney cheers up any curry and can also be added to soup (see p.47).

Stock cubes:
Although normally I advocate making your own batches of stock, when cooking for yourself you do not always have the time or inclination . . . so fall back on these when desperate.

Herbs and spices:
Buy as many different kinds as possible: basil and oregano for tomato dishes; black peppercorns to be freshly ground and salt for occasional use; cinnamon, cloves and nutmeg for sweet and savoury dishes.

Food essences:
Rose water (you can now buy this in supermarkets), almond and vanilla essences.

Tip: Make your own vanilla sugar by filling a jar with (home-ground) caster sugar and pushing in a couple of vanilla pods. Just add more sugar as it gets used up. The pods keep almost indefinitely.

Miscellaneous:
Tinned tuna; cocoa powder.

4
MEAN CUISINE

Bringing home the harvest is only part of the story. It doesn't matter how penny-pinching you or I have been, we can still upset the apple cart if we believe that that is all there is to money-saving. It isn't.

WASTE

Everytime we buy something and then throw part of it away – it's money lost. It truly is. No-one gives us anything for free. Even the freebie in the Kornflakes is costed into the Krispies. But not all waste is packaging. Let me tell you about a discovery I made several years ago. One day, after preparing the family meal, I decided to weigh all the leaves and peelings that I was intending to chuck away and was shattered to find they were one-fifth of the original weight of the vegetables. This meant that out of every £5 I was spending on food (it's not only vegetables that have waste) I could be throwing up to £1's worth into the bin. More if the family didn't clear their plates.

At that time I was spending about £20 a week on food (to feed six, a dog, and occasionally Grandma) and filling two dustbins a week (not all with food but you get the picture). This meant I could be disposing of at least £200 of waste a year. It simply did not make economic sense – even I could see that. But what could I do?

Fate (as usual) took a hand. A day or two later I picked up a magazine and read about Chef Jean Conil who could serve up meals for a week on what most people normally throw away. And he explained how he did it: using outer leaves (which have umpteen more vitamins and flavour than anything in the middle) and keeping all trimmings for the stockpot. Not even a bone was thrown.

Being at the impressionable age of 38 (it's never too late to learn) I followed Jean's example. It's no good reading about hints and tips and then not putting them into practice, and anyway I wanted to see if I could do better. From then on, in our house, waste became the Eighth Deadly Sin.

Just because you are shopping or cooking for one doesn't mean you waste little. Not as much obviously in comparison with a family's waste but it could still be around one-fifth. Especially if you are a convenience foodie.

The potential

Now the less money we have to spend on food the more important it is to use every bit to its full potential. During 'The Challenge' I tried hard to avoid buying anything that had obvious waste and so I wasn't expecting much to be thrown away. Got it right for once! Or had I?

In fact there turned out to be lots of things that I could have disposed of. So I needed to find a use for them to justify the expenditure. Usually I jot down details when recycling together with the approximate amount of money saved. This is fun to tot up each week and totalling at the end of the year is bliss because it could run into three figures. Then you can quite honestly say out loud what a clever girl (or boy) you've been.

Would you believe that, if The Challenge was carried on over a full year it would be quite possible for one person to save at least £150 through recycling? And that's without adding all the other forms of saving: the money-off coupons, the free offers, the home-grown and the home-made, and walking to the next bus stage ... At the very least it would pay for a holiday. Everything is worth doing when you have an objective.

Here are some notes taken from my Day Book during the four-week period. I hope they encourage you to try some recycling for yourself.

Meat/fish
- Simmered chicken bone in water with veg. trimmings (onion, celery, carrot). After removing bone blended remainder for soup (20p).
- Simmered fish skins, bones, tails with a bit of onion and lemon rind. Strained and used for fish stock (10p).
- Saved bacon fat for frying and making pastry and oatcakes.
- Removed skin from chicken. Grilled until golden and crisp. Snipped over salad for garnish and flavour.
- Cooked shin beef in plenty of water until very tender. Used meat for main dishes, but kept the gravy for soup (French onion, p.110) and to add to mince beef (30p).

Dairy
- Used rinsed milk cartons for freezing fish and meat stocks, also soups.
- Used margarine and yogurt tubs for pudding moulds and to store home-made yogurt. Also for seed pots. Useful too for freezing small quantities.
- Used clear plastic egg cartons for freezing small amounts: tomato purée, stock, ice cubes, cream.
- Egg shells: crushed and used to clarify stock. Can also be dug into the ground if you have a garden. And (a tip sent to me) upturn egg shells to allow more white to drain out. Use for glazing pastry etc.

Fruit/Vegetables:
- Used outer leaves of lettuce, cabbage, Chinese leaves for soups, dolmas, and for lining terrines (see p.112).
- Cut free the stiff ribs of lettuce and Chinese leaves and steamed them. Braised them in butter and ate as mock asparagus (25p).
- Grated cores of cabbage and Chinese leaves for coleslaw (5p).
- Steamed vegetables above main meal to save fuel.

- Used celery leaves in salads and shredded stump for stews and stir-fried vegetables (10p).
- Potatoes eaten baked or, if new, boiled in skins to avoid peelings.
- Apple peelings – ate 'em!
- Lemon shells: filled with fish paté (entertaining). Grated peel for flavouring. Soaked shells in water and used for cooking rice (see p.32)/fish stock/as a hair rinse.

Groceries
- Cereal cartons: used as 'bin liners'. Waxed paper inners: used for baking (5p).
- Supermarket carrier bags: used as bin liners.
- Juice cartons: used to freeze liquids.
- Coffee jars: used for storing dry goods.
- Vinegar bottles: saved for home-made wine and herb vinegars (see pp.119, 129), cordials, syrups (40p).
- Honey jars: saved for home-made preserves (40p).
- Small tubs, jelly and tea packets, plastic dried milk 'bottles' – anything safe – collected and stuffed firmly with old newspaper and resealed. Made a very good 'shop' present for my grandchild (£1.00).

Memo: It's never worth hoarding things if you're not going to use them. Once upon a time I could open cupboard doors and hundreds of little yogurt tubs would come tumbling out. Eventually I got fed up of putting them all back, kept ten and threw the rest away. And felt very much better.

FUEL-SAVING

Cooking for a large family I've always been used to filling the oven and sometimes even wished I had two. But when it came to cooking for myself alone it just didn't seem worth the trouble and certainly not the expense of turning on the oven to cook one thing. I've heard others say the same.

The Oven

The thing to do is plan your cooking to take the utmost advantage of the oven each time it's on. Not everything has to be eaten the day it's made so above the main dish you could be baking a tray of biscuits or some cakes. On the lower shelf you could be cooking a pudding.

☆ *If you really only want to cook one thing then fill the remaining space with casseroles half full of nothing but water. Use this when hot for any cooking you need to do on top of the oven (such as rice), or use it for washing up or hand washing. But please be very very careful how you carry the steaming pots.*

You can even store surplus hot water (from kettle or oven) in vacuum flasks for later use.

There's nothing worse than being faced with the same food day after day. This often happens when it seems more economical and less trouble to make a large dish of something rather than just a single helping. But by using one batch of pastry, a Yorkshire pudding tin (the type with four sections) and a selection of fillings you can cook four different things all at the same time – one to eat on the day, others that will keep.

Suggestions for fillings:

Cooked shin beef in thickened gravy with vegetables
Flaked smoked fish with cooked rice and vegetables in Mustard sauce (p.114)
Chicken in a velouté sauce (p.18) with vegetables
Bacon, cheese and tomato quiche (p.96)
Onion and apple flan (p.60)
Apple and sultana pie
Apple dumpling
Apricot pie
Bakewell tart
Clafoutis (p.95)

The hob

A great deal can be cooked by using only the hob – this
has the advantage of being both speedy and controllable,
and I found I was able to cook several things at the same
time using just one heating element – and a couple of
steamers.

Although I've been steaming for years I've only just
discovered an interesting fact. Animal protein and
vegetables don't need the same cooking temperature.

Animal proteins are best cooked at a temperature
slightly *below* boiling point. This is why meat cooks so
beautifully in a slow cooker (while the vegetables remain
underdone) and an egg will continue to cook even though
the heat has been turned out.

79

Vegetable proteins, on the other hand (particularly root crops), are best cooked at a temperature *higher* than boiling point. This is not impossible. You can either:

- use a pressure cooker
  (well worth the money)
- cook them in the oven
  (at the same time as the main dish)
- cook them by steaming them over an ordinary saucepan containing fast-boiling water.
  (The temperature rises slightly as the steam condenses.)

My husband (who seems to know *everything*) tells me that if you add an impurity to water (even a pinch of salt) it will raise the boiling point slightly. So it makes even more sense to cook something in the bottom pan while you steam something else above it.

☆ *When steaming, wrap different flavoured foods in loose foil parcels to keep the flavours separate. Pack loosely to allow steam to circulate.*

☆ *For foods that cook quickly – fish, liver, sliced apples – do not use the second steamer. Place the food on a heatproof shallow dish and cover with foil to keep in the steam. Place on top of the bottom steamer or over a pan of boiling water.*

☆ *Try to take advantage of the heat at the top of the steamer and steam some fish ready for a fish pie the next day or some fruit for a pudding.*

If you don't want to be bothered with the large steamers, then do invest in one of the folding fit-in-any-pan type. These are perfect for small portions and mine (covered with a doily) doubles as a cake plate.

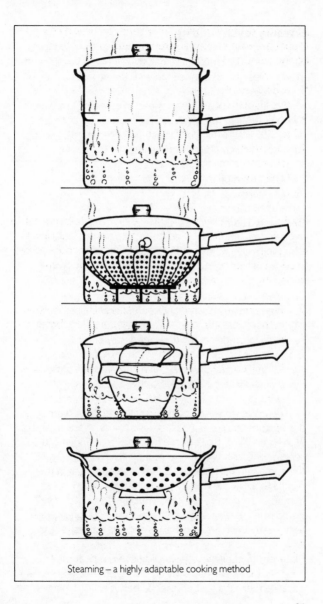

Steaming – a highly adaptable cooking method

Savoury layer pudding

This is the type of pudding that is a winner for those cold winter days. Because of its small scale it could be steamed in an ordinary lidded saucepan with the vegetables cooking in the water alongside.

For this you need suet. Instead of investing in a packet which you might not often use try asking your butcher when you are buying your meat for one or two ounces of suet fat which you can shred yourself.

2oz (50g) plain flour
1oz (25g) shredded suet
½ teaspoon baking powder
Pinch mixed herbs

Filling suggestions:
Chopped onion/2oz (50g) bacon pieces/1oz (25g) grated cheese
Chopped onion/1 skinned sausage/dash brown sauce
Left-over cooked savoury minced meat or shin beef

Put all the ingredients for the suet pastry into a basin. Gently stir in enough cold water to make a soft dough. Knead lightly on a floured surface until smooth. Divide dough into three pieces, each one a little bigger than the last.

Take the smallest piece of dough and roll it out to fit the bottom of a *small* greased basin (or large tea-cup). Top with some filling. Roll out the next piece of dough and repeat. Finish off with the largest piece of dough. Cover the container with greased paper, folding a pleat in the centre to allow for rising. Tie with string. Steam for 45 minutes – remember to keep checking the water level. Remove the paper and turn the pudding out onto a dish. Serve with a rich gravy or sauce and vegetables in season.

Many people believe you should never re-heat cooked meat. Actually it all depends on what you mean by re-heat because there is a vast difference between 'warming up' a pre-cooked meat dish and re-cooking it. When you 'warm-up' food the temperature is not high enough to kill any bacteria it may contain and the gentle heat can positively encourage them to flourish. *So never warm-up meat dishes.*

On the other hand 're-cooking' means applying the same conditions that you would do if the meat were raw and giving it ample time to heat right through (at least 25 minutes for a one-person portion) at a high temperature. Steaming is ideal for this.

TAKE A BASIC MIX

The main problem with having only one mouth to feed is that when it comes to baking in bulk you could end up eating nothing but ginger biscuits for *weeks*. On the other hand, as I've said before, you have to grab the opportunity to fill the oven every time it is on. That way it needn't be on so often. More pennies in the piggy bank.

If all this seems like continual hard labour then rest assured – it needn't be. The trick is to have something ready to draw upon when you have a gap to fill. So – take a basic mix . . .

Scones, biscuits and cakes

Baking your own tea-time and coffee-break snacks is not only cheaper than buying them, it is also more satisfying and, of course, the home-baked variety always tastes better.

Here is a fairly basic scone recipe where I've substituted dried milk for the fresh. All you need do is add water to make up the amount you need plus something extra if you wish. Sultanas maybe, or a little grated cheese if you fancy something savoury. It's far nicer to have one or two freshly baked scones to eat than be left with three or four that have gone stale.

Basic scone mix

8oz (250g) plain flour
4 teaspoons baking powder
1 rounded tablespoon dried milk powder
1oz (25g) sugar
2oz (50g) margarine

Sift together the flour, baking powder and milk powder. Stir in the sugar and rub in the margarine until the mixture is like fine crumbs. Store in an air-tight container in the fridge for up to a month.

   To bake: To each rounded tablespoon of mixture add 2 tablespoons of water and mix to a soft dough. This will make two scones. Either roll out and cut with a scone cutter (looks neater) or form into two balls and roll each out to about ½ inch (1 cm) thick.

   Place on a greased and floured or non-stick baking sheet and either brush with a little milk/spare egg white to glaze or leave plain. Bake for about 10 minutes (or until brown) at a temperature as near as possible to gas mark 7, 425°F (220°C), preferably at the top of the oven. Cool on a wire rack.

Basic biscuit mix

This uncooked biscuit mixture keeps well in the fridge for up to two weeks, longer if kept in the freezer. Cut off a few slices to bake whenever you've the oven on for something else. If you make more than one variation you can cook a mixed batch.

3oz (75g) butter
3oz (75g) margarine
4oz (125g) sugar, preferably caster
1 egg yolk or part (optional but makes a richer biscuit)
8oz (250g) plain flour
½ teaspoon baking powder

Cream together the butter, margarine and sugar, beat in the egg (if using). Sift together the flour and baking powder and work into the creamed mixture. Knead gently, then form into rolls about 2 inches (5cm) in diameter. Wrap in waxed paper or cling-film and chill thoroughly or freeze.

To bake: Cut into thin slices about 1/4 inch (0.5cm) thick and bake on a greased baking sheet at gas mark 4, 350°F (180°C) for about 10 minutes or until golden.

Variations
- Add a few finely chopped dried apricots or prunes to the dry ingredients.
- Add grated lemon rind when creaming the fat.
- Add 2 teaspoons dried ginger or instant coffee powder to the flour.

☆ *If the temperature of the oven is not exactly right for scones and biscuits, then gain a few extra degrees by baking on the highest shelf.*

Basic cake mixture

I found cake mixtures to be too fiddly to cut down to single portions so I got around this problem by making up the full amount and then turning the mixture into four different things. This worked very well with a little advance planning so that they would fit into the menu.

4oz (125g) plain flour
1 teaspoon baking powder
4oz (125g) sugar, preferably caster
4oz (125g) margarine
2 eggs

Sift together the flour and baking powder. Cream together the sugar and margarine. Stir in a little flour, then beat in the eggs. Fold in the rest of the flour. Use the mixture in the following ways.

One-tin sandwich cake

This is a way to make half a cake which is an acceptable amount for one person. All you do is cook half the Basic cake mixture in one sponge cake tin at gas mark 5, 375°F (190°C) for 25 minutes. After cooling cut in half. Cover one half with filling, then top with the other.

Suggested fillings:
Lemony apple curd (p.105)
Apricot purée (see below)
Blackberry butter (p.133)
Buttercream

Apricot purée

3oz (75g) dried apricots
5fl oz (150ml) hot water
2 teaspoons honey

Soak the apricots overnight in the water with the honey stirred in. The next day put everything into a pan and heat slowly. Simmer until the apricots are soft and the liquid syrupy. Liquidise and leave to cool. Cover and store in the fridge for up to a week. Use as a cake or pie filling or to top a steamed pudding.

Steamed lemon pudding

Although it's normal to cook and bake a cake mixture immediately after preparing it I've found that, once assembled and covered, this little pudding will sit happily for several hours before you steam it and still turn out light and fluffy.

Grease a large tea-cup and put 2 teaspoons of Lemony apple curd (p.105), honey or Blackberry butter (p.133) in the base. Half fill the cup with Basic cake mixture (you'll need about ¼ of the quantity given on p.85), cover with greased pleated paper and fasten with string or a large rubber band. Steam for 30 minutes. Turn out onto a dish and eat with custard.

Bakewell tart
This traditional tart is flavoured with almonds, and perfect for baking in those four-section Yorkshire pudding tins (see p.79).

Line the tin with shortcrust pastry and spread with jam. Use ¼ of the Basic cake mixture and beat in a drop of almond essence. Spread this over the jam and scatter over a few flaked almonds. Bake at gas mark 6, 400°F (200°C) for about 20 minutes until the mixture has set.

Lemony variation:
During The Challenge I had no almonds or jam so I spread the pastry with Lemony apple curd (p.105) and flavoured the cake mixture with grated lemon rind. Cook as above.

Apple variation:
Peel, core and thickly slice 1 dessert apple. Fold into the cake mixture and spoon into the pastry case. Cook as above.

Upside-down apricot pudding
Soak 2 dried apricots overnight in a teacup of water. Put the soaked apricots in a small pan with 1 dessertspoon of sugar and 2 tablespoons of the soaking liquid. Simmer to reduce the liquid to a syrup.

Grease a very small frying-pan with butter. Pour the apricots and syrup into the pan and spread a quarter of the Basic cake mixture (p.85) on top. Cover with foil and cook over a moderate heat for 10 minutes. Turn out onto a hot dish and serve immediately.

Alternatively, use a small heatproof dish and cook in the oven for 15–20 minutes at gas mark 4, 350°F (180°C).

Small amounts of left-over mixture can be used for fairy cakes: plain or fruit (add a few sultanas) or could be spread in a greased and floured shallow baking tin and cooked as a slab. Use for an individual trifle or this better-than-average dessert:

Orange and banana layer

1 pkt orange jelly
5fl oz (150ml) hot water
5fl oz (150ml) fresh orange juice
½–1 banana
1 small tin (6oz/170g) evaporated milk
Cooked sponge cake

Dissolve the jelly in a little of the hot water, then add the rest of the water and the orange juice.

Using a deep oblong tin (e.g. a loaf tin) pour in a little jelly and leave to set. Cover with sliced banana and carefully spoon over enough jelly to hold the slices in place (too much and they float). Leave to set.

Meanwhile make a mousse by whipping the evaporated milk until thick and then beating in the remainder of the just-setting jelly. Pour over the banana base. Finish with a slab of sponge cake cut to fit the tin. Chill well.

To serve: Run a knife around the inside edge of the tin to loosen filling. Dip the tin *briefly* in hot water and turn out onto a plate. Cut into slices.

☆ *Save up for good-quality non-stick bakeware. This cuts down on the amount of fat you'll need to use when baking.*

Pastry

Once upon a time I always bought my pastry ready-made and frozen. No matter what I did to it, it came up trumps. Although my mother and my daughter made perfect pastry, I never could. They tried to help and encouraged me to work alongside them, following every step. Yet although we used the same ingredients, the same method and the same oven, theirs was always melt-in-the-mouth and mine was breeze-blocks. Improvement only came when I used more fat in proportion to flour than is usually recommended.

My basic shortcrust pastry

12oz (350g) plain flour
8oz (250g) margarine
Iced water to mix

Put the flour in a basin and rub in the margarine until the mixture looks like crumbs. Sprinkle in a little water and mix with a knife. Keep adding water sparingly until the mixture binds together but is not sticky.

Turn out on a floured board and knead together very gently until you have a smooth light dough. Chill for at least 15 minutes before rolling out.

☆ *I find 1 teaspoon of water per ounce (25g) of flour is about the right amount for shortcrust, but flours do vary and you may need to add a drop or two more. The most important thing is to use very cold water and add it slowly so that you don't overdo it.*

Pastry can be made much more exciting when you add a touch of flavour. A hint of mixed spice for a fruit pie. Or ginger with beef. When a friend of mine first introduced me to lemon pastry I was completely bowled over and it inspired me so much I rushed home to try other variations. She simply added grated lemon rind to the dry pastry ingredients and made it up in the normal way. It tastes gorgeous with apples, and also with fish. If that works why not grated orange zest with beef or apricots . . .?

Yeast dough

If you don't normally make bread then this is the one time I recommend using a packet mix. There's really no point in laying out for a packet of strong plain flour and dried yeast if you don't intend using them often. Make the most of a mix and you won't be out of pocket.

Enriched bread dough

To an ordinary 10oz (300g) packet mix add ½oz (15g) melted butter and 2 teaspoons egg yolk (see p.25). Make up with water as directed but use fractionally less than the instructions say because of the egg.
Note: enriched dough takes a little longer to rise.

Chelsea buns   *Makes 6*

Using half the enriched dough, roll out thinly on a floured board. Brush the dough with melted butter, sprinkle over a little sugar and some sultanas. Roll the dough up like a Swiss roll and cut into 6 slices, each 1½ inches (3.5cm) thick. Place the slices flat on a greased baking sheet, leaving room for them to spread. Cover with a thin cloth and leave in a warm spot to rise. When doubled in size bake at gas mark 6, 400°F (200°C) for about 20 minutes or until dark gold. Remove from the oven and brush immediately with sugar syrup (p.91). Leave to cool.

Savarin or babas

Press the remaining half of the enriched bread dough either into 1 large ring mould (savarin) or 3 individual ones (babas) and bake at gas mark 6, 400°F (200°C) for 20 minutes (savarin) or 12 minutes (babas).

While still in the tin and piping hot pour over a little sugar syrup (p.91) and repeat until the dough has taken up enough syrup so that it just about floats in the tin. Leave to cool. Turn out, fill the centre with chopped fruit and serve with thick yogurt or Sweet yogurt dressing (p.49).

Savarins and babas freeze well after the syrup-soaking stage so if you have a freezer it is worth making extra to use them for entertaining, especially if you add a little liqueur to the syrup!

☆ *Buy miniature liqueurs and spirits occasionally with your weekly savings and keep them especially for flavouring desserts or special cakes. Useful ones are: Tia Maria, Cointreau, kirsch, rum, brandy, whisky. (See p.129 for how to make your own liqueurs.)*

Sugar syrup

This is something I *always* have in stock in the fridge. It freezes well too. Make a note of the proportion of sugar to water you used and then every time you find a recipe that needs a syrup solution you have it already made. Just dilute with water as required.

---

1 lb (500g) sugar
10fl oz (300ml) water

Heat the sugar and water slowly in a heavy-bottomed saucepan until the sugar has dissolved. Bring to the boil, then simmer for 4 minutes. Cool and store in sterilised bottles in the fridge. It keeps indefinitely.

Pizza

To half a 10oz (300g) packet of basic bread dough mix add 1 teaspoon sunflower oil, then make up with water in the normal way. Knead well until the dough is smooth, then divide up into 2 or 3 portions. Roll out each to the size of a saucer and spread with home-made Tomato sauce (see below) and top with grated cheese. At this point the pizzas can be frozen.

Bake at gas mark 5, 375°F (190°C) for about 20 minutes until the base is golden and the cheese is bubbling. (If cooking from frozen allow 30 minutes.)

Tomato sauce

This is worth making in bulk and freezing away in small quantities if you can. Use to top pizzas, to accompany pasta, or to add to meat and vegetable dishes. Even if you only have a small freezer compartment at the top of your fridge you can fill an ice cube tray with sauce and just use as many cubes as you need.

1/2 onion, chopped
Sunflower oil
14oz (400g) can tinned tomatoes
1 tablespoon tomato purée
1 teaspoon sugar
Black pepper
1 teaspoon mixed herbs

In a saucepan fry the onion gently in a little oil. Add the tinned tomatoes and juice. Chop the tomatoes up roughly, then stir in the tomato purée. Add the sugar and plenty of freshly ground black pepper. (White pepper just isn't right.) Finally add the herbs (traditionally basil and oregano) and simmer for about half an hour until the sauce has thickened. Cool and store in the fridge for up to 3 days or freeze.

Pitta bread

Pitta bread is traditionally made in flat oval shapes which can be opened out into 'pockets' when cut in half. Stuff the pockets with crisp shredded salad and a hot or cold savoury filling such as Chilli con carne (p.45), Re-fried beans (p.29) or small chunks of grilled chicken or fish and you

have a meal for one in itself. Torn into pieces the bread can also be used with savoury dips for entertaining.

To make 3 breads, use half a 10oz (300g) packet of white or brown bread mix, and make up in the normal way. Divide into 3 pieces and roll out each piece into an oblong. Brush with melted butter, fold over and, either by hand or with a rolling pin, flatten and shape into an oval about 7 inches (18cm) long and ¼ inch (0·5cm) thick. Cover with a cloth and leave to rest for 20 minutes.

Place the breads on greased baking sheets and bake for 10 minutes at gas mark 6, 400°F (200°C). *Do not over-cook.* Cool on a wire rack covered with a cloth to keep them soft. Store in a polythene bag, or freeze.

To reheat, hold a bread briefly under the cold tap, then pop it under a hot grill for a couple of minutes on each side. The water helps the bread puff up and keeps it soft and moist.

The versatile triple-act: eggs, milk and flour

Preparing a basic mix in bulk and varying what you do with it doesn't have to stop with dry ingredients. The versatile combination of eggs, milk and flour can also help you get variety into your diet without spending a fortune.

Let's start with just the eggs and milk. These are the basic ingredients for many dishes and it's worth taking time out to understand how they work together. Not every recipe needs the same proportions but it is possible to begin with one concentration, such as 2 eggs and ¼ pint (150ml) milk, use half of that for an individual flan and then, by adding more milk, carry on to make a custard.

When you add flour to this basic combination the mixture becomes a batter. At normal strength you can use it for pancakes, Yorkshire pudding, Toad in the hole and Clafoutis (p.95). Then, by adding more flour, a raising agent and sugar to the remainder you can make drop scones.

Guide to proportions

	Eggs	Milk	Plain flour	Sugar	Other
Quiche	2	¼ pint (150 ml)	–	–	–
Egg custard	2–3	½ pint (300 ml)	–	1 oz (25 g)	–
Pouring custard	1–2	½ pint (300 ml)	–	1 oz (25 g)	–
Pancake batter	1	¼ pint (150 ml)	2 oz (50 g)	–	–
Yorkshire pudding	1	½ pint (300 ml)	4 oz (125 g)	–	–
Drop scones	1	¼ pint (150 ml)	4 oz (250 g)	1 oz (25 g)	1½ tsp baking powder
Coating batter	2	¼ pint (150 ml)	4 oz (125 g)	–	2 tsp cooking oil

Opposite is a guide to the proportions needed for different things and a brief method for each. Use this to help you get the most of what you have available. For example, if you only have 1 egg left for your main meal add half a pint of milk. Use half the liquid to make an individual Yorkshire pudding or to top a mini-casserole (see p.116) and use the other half for a pouring custard to have with your pudding. Make it in a measuring jug so that you can read off how much you have left. As long as you remember what proportion of eggs to milk you used you can adjust the amount of flour or sugar you need to add accordingly.

Toad in the hole

This good old English classic is a perfect way to use up one sausage and about 4fl oz (115ml) pancake batter.

Split the sausage in half lengthwise and lay the halves side by side in a small baking tin. Cook for 10 minutes at gas mark 6, 400°F (200°C). Drain off any fat and immediately pour the batter over the sausages. Bake for a further 20–30 minutes until the batter has puffed up and is golden brown.

Variation: If you have any beef in gravy left over from a casserole make yourself a single batter pudding and pour the thoroughly re-heated meat and juices over the top (see pp.82–83).

Variation: This batter is also good for a sweet pudding. Butter an ovenproof dish and cover the base with a layer of sliced banana or apple wedges tossed in sugar. Pour over the batter and cook as above. If you use stoned cherries instead this makes the traditional French dish *Clafoutis.*

Basic quiches and flans

Strictly speaking a quiche is made with eggs and cream and a flan is made with eggs and milk, though the words are fairly interchangeable nowadays. I've also successfully used eggs and yogurt.

The proportions are 2 eggs to 5fl oz (150ml) of liquid, beaten together. This is poured into an uncooked pastry case over the filling of your choice. The more filling you have, the less egg mixture you need to fill the case. Bake at gas mark 5–6, 375°–400°F (190°–200°C) for 20–30 minutes until golden and set.

Filling suggestions:
Fried bacon pieces, grated cheese, sliced tomato
Sweetcorn and cubed ham
Sweetcorn and chopped peppers
Sliced mushroom and ham
Chopped fresh herbs
Onion and apple (see p.60)
Cooked diced vegetables
Smoked fish and cheese

☆ *If using a bottomless flan ring or – for individual flans – muffin rings, place it on the base of a baking sheet (by this I mean turn the sheet upside down). With no rim to get in the way it's then easy to slide things off. Bear this in mind when baking anything that could easily break.*

The egg

It's truly amazing how far one egg will go if you give it the chance. Previously I'd always worked on the theory that a little too much egg wouldn't really make all that difference. And wasn't it good for me anyway?

This means that during my life-span (to date) I've probably gone through a hundred dozen more eggs than I needed to. Money down the cholesterol-clogged drain again.

Although I had enough food to eat during The Challenge without needing to 'manufacture' much, it was really nice to be able to make just one or two (well, five or six) little treats to improve my lot. And all these were made with *part* of an egg.

A reminder:
- 1 whole grade 2 egg will measure out to 4 *table*spoonsful.
- 1 grade 2 egg *yolk* will measure out to 4 *tea*spoonsful.

Mayonnaise
How good to be able to have the real thing without needing to make more than a one-person portion.

5fl oz (150ml) sunflower oil
2 teaspoons egg yolk
Pinch mustard powder (optional)
1 teaspoon vinegar or lemon juice

Blend the oil into the yolk, drop by drop, stirring all the time. When the yolk thickens add the oil a little faster but never stop stirring. Finally stir in the mustard powder (if using) and the vinegar or lemon juice.

 Blend mayonnaise with an equal quantity of yogurt – this makes it less rich. It also goes further!

Cheese straws
Because the standard recipe makes an awful lot of these tasty snacks, I have devised a version which makes good use of spare egg yolk and left-over tomato purée and cheese – which all goes to show that the tiniest bits of things need never be wasted.

These keep well in an air-tight tin and are very good as nibbles for yourself (cheaper than scoffing a packet of crisps) or to hand round when entertaining.

97

2oz (50g) plain flour
Pepper
1oz (25g) margarine
1oz (25g) Cheddar cheese, grated
2 teaspoons egg yolk
1/4 teaspoon tomato purée
1–2 teaspoons water

Put the flour and a good grind or pinch of pepper in a bowl and rub in the margarine. Stir in the cheese, then add the egg yolk, tomato purée and a little water to bind to a stiff dough.

Roll out on a floured board to a thickness of 1/4 inch (1/2cm). Cut into narrow finger-lengths strip. Leave flat or twist into corkscrews. Lay on a greased baking sheet and bake for 10–15 minutes at gas mark 6, 400°F (200°C) until pale gold.

Note: These cook well in the oven if put in as soon as the heat has been turned off after cooking another dish at gas mark 5, 375°F (190°C) or higher. Leave for 10–20 minutes.

☆ Eggs are high in cholesterol. Reduce your intake by boiling, frying or poaching a smaller grade (6 or 7) rather than a standard one. (But when baking be aware that most recipes require a standard (2 or 3) egg.)

Poor Knights of Windsor

This is so traditional you can almost feel yourself back in Tudor times as you munch your way through it.

1 tablespoon milk
1/2 teaspoon honey
1 egg yolk
2 small slices brown bread, cut in fingers
Butter or sunflower oil for frying
Extra honey for serving

Blend the milk with the honey and beat into the egg yolk. Dip the bread strips into this mixture and fry in butter or oil (or a mixture of both) until the bread fingers are crisp and golden. Eat hot with more honey and/or yogurt spooned over.

When I began to use only part of an egg in my recipes I needed to find uses for the remainder. This wasn't too difficult as many things are lifted out of the mean cuisine into the almost haute by the addition of egg. Strange, isn't it, that when you begin to be really frugal, standards improve. Many of the recipes in this book use only part of an egg, so the easy way to make your eggs go further is to pick a combination of dishes that will use up whole eggs. When this doesn't suit the situation you can use left-over egg in these ways:

Whole egg or egg yolk
- for enriching pastry
- to add to mashed potato
- for binding burgers, stuffings and croquettes
- for glazing pastry
- for coating fish and chicken

Egg yolk only
- for thickening sauces
- for making Mayonnaise (p.97) or Hollandaise sauce (see below)

Egg white only
- for meringues
- for glazing pastry
- for sorbets (p.117)

Hollandaise sauce
This luxurious-tasting sauce is traditionally eaten with asparagus or salmon, but I use it to 'dress up' any steamed vegetables or fish.

1oz (25g) butter
2 teaspoons egg yolk
Juice of ½ lemon or 1 dessertspoon vinegar

Melt the butter in a tea-cup in a pan of hot water. Take the cup away from the heat and allow to cool slightly, then stir in the egg yolk. Replace the cup in the hot water and stir continuously with a small fork until thickened. Blend in the lemon juice or vinegar and serve at once.

Mousseline sauce
Add one part stiffly whipped cream or evaporated milk to two parts Hollandaise sauce. Mix well and season with pepper to taste. Serve with steamed vegetables or fish.

Mean Cuisine it may be, but 'A penny saved is a penny earned' as it says on my little money box. By not wasting food and being tight with the fuel I can now afford to buy something else. Now *that's* luxury!

5
INCREDIBLE EDIBLES

In the past most of my culinary projects have been geared to how much a dish or meal would cost. Could I make a four-course meal for eight people for £2 total? A dessert for six for under 30p? Things like that.

With The Four-week Challenge the emphasis was different. Once I'd spent my budget each week what I had to do was to make what I'd bought into seven days' worth of meals that were interesting enough to eat. Some people, looking at my shopping lists, might think that that must have been extremely difficult. Well, read on.

Putting it all together

If you've ever watched children playing with Lego bricks you'll see the fun they get from putting them together, making first one thing and then another. That's creativity. I get the same pleasure in my kitchen when I'm putting together different ingredients. That's the delightful thing about food – given the same ingredients we seem to be able to come up with endless variations. No two people think alike.

This was proved when we ran a competition during the BBC TV series *The Goode Kitchen*. We asked for ideas for a two-course meal to feed four people which could either be a starter and a main course, or the main dish and a pudding. The ingredients were to be the same for everyone: 6oz (175g) chicken or fish, 5fl oz (150ml) yogurt, 1 egg, ½ lemon, 4oz (125g) oatmeal, herbs and seasonings – plus anything else the contestant wished to add to the value of 50p. Not a lot you could do with that, you might think. Don't you believe it. There were an incredible number of entries, no two the same and all very, very good.

So – don't assume that basic ingredients can only result in basic meals. My dishes during The Challenge varied from the ordinary-but- tasty to the downright-unusual-but- delicious. Some of the following recipes are examples of this and I'll leave each to tell its own story.

The Cross-bread

This is worthy of a long introduction because it really is an exceptional 'dish' that can be made from almost any source of protein plus a little flour. It is a true hybrid, being a cross between a burger and a chapati, and originated the day I was expecting a visitor but had only one sausage and not a lot else. What seemed hardly enough to feed one made a very pleasant snack for two. Because it is so speedy to make I was even able to demonstrate it from start to finish on a local radio programme and the presenter ate it with genuine relish. You can choose whichever protein and seasonings you have available so there are endless variations. I've even made it with half a cup of left-over Chilli con carne (p.45). The proportions are flexible but never use less protein than the weight of flour – up to twice as much, if possible.

The cross-bread – sausage version

1 large (2oz/50g) uncooked sausage
1 dessertspoon grated onion
Pinch dried mixed herbs or dash of brown sauce
2oz (50g) plain flour
Water to bind
Sunflower oil for frying
Shredded lettuce
1oz (25g) grated cheese

Remove the skin from the sausage and mash the sausagemeat with a fork. Work in the onion, seasoning and flour and a little water to bind.

Knead the mixture by hand until it is well blended (allow 2–5 minutes depending upon the type of meat used). Divide into two equal portions and roll each out very thinly on a very well floured board. Lift one 'pancake' carefully with a fish slice and fry it in hot oil about ¼ inch (0.5cm) deep for about 1 minute. Turn and cook the other side for a further minute. Transfer to kitchen paper to drain while you're cooking the second 'pancake'. While still warm, fill each 'cross-bread' with shredded lettuce, and grated cheese and roll up. Serve garnished with tomato wedges.

Cross-bread variations:
Using the same method try these alternatives to the sausage:
2oz (50g) cooked minced beef plus a pinch of chilli powder
2oz (50g) cooked red beans plus 1 egg yolk
2oz (50g) canned baked beans plus 1 egg yolk
2oz (50g) cooked red lentils plus 1 egg yolk and 1oz (25g) grated cheese

Stir-fry sauce

This was devised at the end of Week 1 when I was using up the bits and bobs of vegetables plus one sausage to make a stir-fry.

2 tablespoons vinegar
1 tablespoon water
1 rounded tablespoon sugar
1 heaped teaspoon tomato purée

Put the first three ingredients into a pan and heat gently until the sugar has dissolved. Blend in the tomato purée, then bring to the boil. The consistency should be thickish. Serve over stir-fried vegetables or with gougons of chicken or fish (p.113).

Yogurt shake

This was 'invented' the day I craved for something sweet yet sharp to follow a spicy dish. I remembered an Indian drink called *lassi* which is made with yogurt and spices and decided to make my own version. The flavouring I tried was a little Lemony apple curd. Would it work? It did – and it was smashing. I've tried using other flavours since but none tastes as good. Got it right first time for once!

2 tablespoons thick yogurt (see p.49)
1 dessertspoon Lemony apple curd (see opposite)
5fl oz (150g) iced water

Beat together the yogurt and the lemony curd, then *very slowly* beat in the iced water. You can do this either with a hand whisk or using a liquidiser. Pour into a tall glass. Instead of drinking it right away I prefer to chill it in the fridge for an hour or so as it seems to thicken slightly.

Beanburgers

I first made these with canned baked beans, then later with home-cooked red kidney beans. Both tasted good and were an interesting way of using vegetable protein.

2 heaped tablespoons baked beans
1 dessertspoon grated onion (more if you like)
2 tablespoons beaten egg (½ egg)
2 slices brown bread, crumbed
Shake of pepper
Flour for coating
Sunflower oil for frying

Mash the baked beans with the onion and stir in the egg and crumbs. Season with pepper. (If too dry add a little sauce from the can of beans, plain water or a dash of brown sauce.) Shape into 2 big burgers. Coat with flour, then fry in medium hot oil for about 1–2 minutes each side until golden. Drain on kitchen paper.

ENTERTAINING

I'd invited four friends round to tea on the first Sunday –
something I had completely forgotten about when I
shopped. (Not that there was much I could afford to do
about it anyway, after all it was only the second day of the
first week!) Nevertheless I wasn't intending to ruin my
reputation by serving just a cuppa and a cream cracker so I
had to put on my thinking cap. I knew with my few basics I
should be able to make something. So I did.

This is what was served:

Sunday Tea
Grated cheese and lettuce sandwiches
Smoked mackerel pâté (p.23) with cream crackers
Bacon, cheese and tomato quiche (p.96)
Drop scones (p.94) with Lemony apple curd (*below*)
Orange jelly mousse (p.106)
Shortbread (p.107)

The marvellous thing about a storecupboard is that once
you've got something in there (even if it's only a little) then
you can make all sorts of things. Nobody realised it was
frugal food at all!

Lemony apple curd
A really lovely country recipe which is far nicer than the
very rich traditional lemon curd. Normally I would prefer
to use cooking apples but at the time I had only Golden
Delicious, so used these instead. It was still good.

2 medium-sized crisp apples, thinly peeled and cored
1 tablespoon water
1 lemon
1oz (25g) concentrated butter
4oz (125g) caster sugar
1 egg

Slice the apples, put them in a pan with the water and cook gently until very soft. Press through a sieve or mash to a pulp with a wooden spoon. Transfer to a small heatproof basin.

Grate the lemon rind and squeeze out the juice. Add both to the apple purée together with the butter, sugar and egg and mix well. (If you have a liquidiser blend the lot together to make a smoother curd.)

Stand the basin over a saucepan of simmering water and stir gently and continuously for about 10 minutes until the mixture thickens. Pour into a small (12oz/350g) sterilised glass jar or two small preserve dishes. Cover and leave to cool. Keep in the fridge.

Note: If you pot up straight into preserve dishes they are ready to bring to the table.

Orange jelly mousse

This was always a family favourite – each week we had a different flavour. It's not worth making a small amount though so keep this recipe for entertaining. However, it will freeze if you can fold in some whipped cream (real or non-dairy) to stabilise the mixture, so at a pinch you could have just one helping.

---

1 pkt orange jelly
5fl oz (150ml) hot water
5fl oz (150ml) fresh orange juice
1 small tin (6oz/170g) evaporated milk, chilled

Dissolve the jelly in the hot water and stir in the orange juice. Cool until just beginning to thicken but not set. Pour the evaporated milk into a large basin and whisk until thickened, then slowly pour in the jelly, still whisking. When thoroughly blended pour into 1 large or 4–6 individual bowls depending on how many you've got coming. Leave to set.

Shortbread

Makes 18 fingers

The cheaper concentrated butter I had bought gave me a
chance to make these luxury biscuits. They really aren't as
good if made with margarine but at a pinch you could use
half and half.

3½oz (100g) concentrated butter
6oz (175g) plain flour
2oz (50g) sugar, preferably caster (see p.72)
1 dessertspoon water

Rub the butter into the flour and add the sugar. Sprinkle
over the water. Using your hands knead everything
together till you have a slightly crumbly dough. Roll out on
a floured board to a thickness of ½ inch (1cm). Transfer to
a greased baking sheet and mark into fingers. Bake at gas
mark 2, 300°F (150°C) for about 40 minutes.

Flapjack

Makes 12

I didn't serve this up to my friends that Sunday, but I could
have done after Week 3 when I bought the ginger. It is a
really delicious version of flapjack which I was able to make
because it doesn't need the syrup I didn't have.

4oz (125g) margarine, or 3oz (75g) concentrated
*   butter plus 1 dessertspoon water*
1 dessertspoon honey
6oz (175g) oatmeal
3oz (75g) sugar
1 teaspoon dried ginger

Beat the margarine or butter/water to a cream. Stir in the
honey. Put the oats, sugar and ginger in a bowl and mix
well. Add the butter and honey mixture and blend well
into the oats. Grease a small square tin (6 × 6 inches/
15 × 15 cm) and press the mixture into the tin. Bake for
20–25 minutes at gas mark 4, 350°F (180°C). Leave in the

tin to cool, then cut into squares. When firm remove from the tin and store in an airtight container. Makes about 12 which should keep you going at tea-time for a bit.

Semolina cake

3oz (75g) soft margarine
3 oz (75g) caster sugar
2 eggs
Grated rind and juice of 1 lemon
3oz (75g) flour
3oz (75g) semolina
2 teaspoons baking powder

Cream the margarine and sugar with the lemon rind until light and fluffy. Beat in the eggs and lemon juice. Sift together the flour, semolina and baking powder and lightly fold this into the creamed mixture.

Turn into a well greased and floured ring mould and bake in the oven at gas mark 4, 350°F (180°C) for 45 minutes. Turn out and cool on a rack.

Dinner-party food

The following recipes are not only good as everyday dishes, they are also suitable to serve up for a dinner party. All are substantial single portions which, when necessary, will divide up into two smaller portions. Many will even make four 'starters'. Best of all they can all be made from the basic weekly purchases I listed in Chapter 3.

The more courses you can serve, the smaller each portion can be and the trick with a dinner party is to present it *à la Nouvelle Cuisine*. This is an extremely attractive way of serving very little. By presenting the food in ingenious and arty arrangements on individual plates (no bowlsful for people to over-help themselves from) you can get away with murder – deliciously. Plan to serve a minimum of four courses. By the time the guests have reached the main dish they'll probably already be feeling more than half-way full. Remind them they still have to leave room for the pudding.

A modern idea (actually it's centuries old – I am fascinated by the history of food and some of my best recipes are medieval) is to serve a sorbet between courses. This refreshes the parts other courses haven't reached. So if you have a freezer try to keep some sorbet in it so that you have an instant dish. A great time-saver.

But just because these recipes are 'suitable for entertaining' doesn't mean you should only make them when you have company. I never have seen the reason why stops should be pulled out only for others. So make them just for yourself too, as often as possible. And there's a very good reason why you should – because practice makes perfect. The easiest way to prepare a perfect meal is to know exactly what should be done and – more importantly – the quickest and best way to do it. And the only way to find that out is by experience – leaving you to enjoy the meal along with everyone else.

Carrot and orange soup

This is a soup I love to make as it gives me a bonus of puréed carrots for a vegetable dish. The soup itself is delightful chilled but, of course, it can also be eaten hot.

3oz (75g) carrots, grated
½ small onion, grated
5fl oz (150ml) chicken stock
5fl oz (150ml) orange juice
½ teaspoon honey
1oz (25g) butter
Pepper to taste
1 tablespoon thick yogurt

Melt the butter in a pan and gently fry the carrots and onions for 5 minutes. Add the stock, orange juice and honey. Bring to the boil and simmer for about 20 minutes until the vegetables are very soft. Cool slightly, then liquidise. Pour the purée through a sieve and press out as much liquid as possible. Use the sieved liquid for soup and the carrot residue in the sieve as a vegetable (hot or cold).

To serve, chill the soup, season with pepper, then blend a little of the yogurt into it to loosen the consistency. Swirl the rest on top of the soup.

Note: the carrot residue can also be used as a topping for cottage pie instead of or with mashed potato.

French Onion Soup
A classic little number this – and very inexpensive, as are most good things.

---

1 small onion (about 4oz/125g), thinly sliced
1oz (25g) butter
1 teaspoon flour
10fl oz (300ml) beef stock
1 bread crust, toasted
1oz (25g) grated cheese

Fry the onion slices in the butter for about 5 minutes, but don't let it colour too much. Sprinkle in the flour and stir. Cook for a further minute, then slowly add the stock, stirring all the time as it thickens. Simmer for 20 minutes.

Meanwhile cut the toasted crust into four pieces and spread grated cheese evenly over each piece. Place three of these in a soup dish (doesn't matter if they overlap) and grill the final piece when the soup is ready. When the cheese is bubbling pour the hot soup over the bread in the bowl and float the final piece on the top.

Stuffed eggs

This is a fancy way to make eggs go further for a starter.
Hardboil 1 egg per person for 10 minutes. Crack the shells
gently and plunge into cold water. Leave to stand for 15
minutes changing the water once after 5 minutes. (This
prevents a black rim forming around the yolk.)

Carefully remove the shells, dry off the eggs and cut
them in half lengthways. Scoop out the yolk and use it for
Kedgeree (p.39) or for mixing with Mayonnaise (p.97) for
egg sandwiches. Fill the cavities with Smoked mackerel
pâté (p.23) and serve with a salad garnish.

Potato gnocchi

Serves 1 for a main meal,
2 for starters

Pronounced 'Nee-ock-ee' (I never serve anything unless I
can say it properly), this is something a little bit different
and very useful when you haven't much in the cupboard.

8oz (250g) cooked potato
1oz (25g) butter or margarine
2 tablespoons beaten egg (see p.25)
2oz (50g) plain flour
Shake of pepper
2oz (50g) grated cheese

Put a large pan ¾ full of water on to boil. Mash the
potatoes with the butter and add the egg and the flour.
Season to taste. Knead thoroughly, adding more flour if
necessary, until you have a firm dough. Form into a long
roll about ½ inch (1cm) thick. Cut into 1 inch (2.5cm)
lengths.

Drop the gnocchi into the boiling water and cook for
about 5–6 minutes. They will rise to the surface when
done. Remove with a slotted spoon and arrange in a
heatproof dish. Cover with grated cheese and put under
the grill to brown. Serve hot with Tomato sauce (p.92).

Chicken and Vegetable Terrine

This is good summer food and a dish I serve often at parties. Once chilled it will cut into 8 or more slices which is not half bad for what it costs.

To line the mould:

Line a small loaf tin with either blanched lettuce or cabbage leaves, strips of bacon or small thin pancakes. Just make sure you have no gaps and you have enough overlap to fold over at the end.

To make the terrine:

1 chicken breast
1 raw sausage (skinned)
2 tablespoons thick yogurt
1/2oz (15g) butter
1 egg white
1 teaspoon powdered gelatine
1 tablespoon hot water
2 large carrots, topped and tailed
Pepper

Cut the carrots lengthways into very thin strips and steam for 2 minutes (see p.81). Cool. Remove the chicken flesh from the bone. Put the flesh into a blender together with the egg white and a shake of pepper and whizz until smooth. Leave to stand in a cold place. Dissolve the gelatine in the water. Melt the butter and stir into the yogurt and whisk both into the chicken mixture. Fold in the dissolved gelatine.

Put some of the chicken mixture into the lined tin and press in a few carrot strips, repeating the layers until the chicken and carrots are used up. Fold over the chosen lining, placing more on top if there are gaps. Cover with folded greaseproof paper, then cooking foil and stand in a baking tin containing about 1 inch (2.5cm) water. Bake for 45 minutes at gas mark 4, 350°F (180°C). Cool in the tin. Chill.

To serve, run a knife between the lining and tin, turn over and shake out the terrine onto a serving dish. Garnish with colourful salad vegetables.

Cherubs on horseback

Serving meat for a 'starter' means you can get away with a meatless main course. The size of the portion depends upon how many you wish to feed – any number from one to four.

1 chicken breast
4 prunes
4 rashers of bacon
5fl oz (150g) chicken stock or wine

Remove the chicken from the bone. Cut the flesh into four chunks. Open out each prune and lay one over each piece of chicken. Wrap a rasher of bacon around each and fasten with a cocktail stick.

Place in a small roasting tin or ovenproof dish and cook near the top of the oven at gas mark 6, 400°F (200°C) for about 30 minutes. Half way through the cooking time add the stock or wine. Serve each cherub, hot or cold, on a nest of rice with a little of the liquid poured over the top.

Goujons of chicken or fish

These are finger strips of chicken or fish (it could also be pork or lamb) which are coated and then deep-fried. Allow about 2oz (50g) per person for a starter and 4oz (125g) for a main course.

All you do is cut the flesh into strips and roll in flour, then dip into beaten egg, making sure all parts are coated. Finally roll in dried breadcrumbs or ... crushed cornflakes!

These can be prepared ahead of time and chilled in the fridge. I then like to give them a second coating of egg and crumbs because it makes them look so much bigger. Deep-fry for about five minutes, then drain and serve on their own, garnished with wedges of tomato, as a starter or accompanied by a substantial crisp green salad for a main course. They also go well with the Stir-fry sauce on p.103.

Hot smoked mackerel in mustard sauce

A fillet of cold smoked mackerel served with a wedge of lemon and a slice of brown bread is an excellent starter in its own right, but this recipe is good if you intend to serve a cold second course.

Allowing 1 smoked mackerel fillet per person, heat the fish by the most convenient method according to whatever else you're cooking, i.e. wrap loosely in foil and steam, bake in a moderate oven, or grill.

Serve on heated plates coated with Mustard sauce (see below) and garnished with a wedge of lemon.

Mustard sauce   *Makes enough for 2 fish fillets*

3oz (75g) butter or margarine
3 dessertspoons water
1 ½ egg yolks (6 teaspoons – see p.25)
1 teaspoon dry mustard
Pepper
1 dessertspoon lemon juice or vinegar

Melt the butter and leave it to cool slightly. Whisk together the water and egg yolks over a low heat until the mixture leaves a trail when the whisk is lifted. Stir the mustard and pepper into the butter, then beat this into the egg mixture a few drops at a time. The sauce will begin to thicken. Stir in the lemon juice or vinegar and serve as soon as possible.

Smoked fish pancakes

For this you need two pancakes per person for a main course which, of course, can be made several days ahead of time. All you do then is prepare the filling on the day and stuff the pancakes. Baking time is short – just long enough for you to lay the table.

Although this recipe uses smoked fish there is absolutely no reason why you shouldn't substitute cooked unsmoked white fish.

Pancake filling

Makes enough for 2 pancakes

6oz (175g) smoked herring or mackerel, flaked
2 tablespoons celery leaves, finely chopped
5fl oz (150ml) Mustard sauce (see opposite)
2 tablespoons Cheddar cheese, grated

Fold the fish and celery leaves into half the mustard sauce
and spread this over each pancake. Roll up loosely and
place in a greased ovenproof dish. Spoon over the
remaining sauce and sprinkle over the cheese. Bake at gas
mark 5, 375°F (190°C) until the pancakes have completely
heated through and the cheese is bubbling (about 15
minutes). Garnish with a bit of greenery if a starter or
serve with a substantial salad if a main course.

Ravioli

Makes 2–3 servings

Make up the basic pasta dough as described on p.70.
Knead well for at least 5 minutes, longer if you can spare
the time. Divide in half, then wrap in greaseproof paper
and leave to stand at room temperature for *at least* 15
minutes. (Two hours is better.) Roll each half out into a
very thin sheet, sprinkling the dough with flour to prevent it
sticking. Cover each sheet with a dry cloth while preparing
the filling.

Meat filling

1 small onion, very finely chopped
1 tablespoon sunflower oil
4oz (125g) minced beef or chicken
2 tablespoons beaten egg
1 tablespoon Cheddar cheese, grated
Pepper

Fry the onion gently in the oil until soft. Add the minced
meat and cook through. Remove the pan from the heat

and beat in the egg, the cheese and a shake of pepper. (If you want a very smooth filling pop the lot in a liquidiser and blend for a few seconds.)

To assemble: Place small dots (about ½ teaspoon) of filling over 1 of the pasta sheets about 1 ¼ inches (3cm) apart in rows. Brush the second sheet of pasta with water and place it, wet side down, over the other. Press down between the 'lumps' with the blunt edge of a knife and then cut through to make little parcels. Check these are well sealed around the edges.

Cook in a large pan of boiling water or meat stock for 7–10 minutes. Drain well and serve in hot buttered soup plates with Tomato sauce (see p.92) and 'mock Parmesan' (p.52).

Bobotie

I first ate Bobotie at a famous hotel in the Lake District where it was made in the traditional way with minced lamb and almonds and seasoned with Indian spices. It made a most unusual starter.

On returning home I tried my own version, this time made with beef, walnuts and dried ginger. It tasted very good so I hope you'll try it. The walnuts aren't essential but if you can find the money for them from your budget that week they do add a certain something.

½oz (15g) butter, or 1 dessertspoon sunflower oil
½ small onion, finely chopped
2 teaspoons tomato purée
4oz (125g) minced beef
1 teaspoon ground ginger
4 dried apricots, soaked overnight
A few chopped walnuts
1 slice brown bread, crumbed
4fl oz (115ml) milk
1 dessertspoon dried milk
1 egg (plus ½ egg yolk if available)

Heat the butter or oil in a frying-pan and gently fry the onions. Add the tomato purée and the minced beef. Sprinkle in the ginger. Cook gently for about 30 minutes, stirring occasionally.

Drain the apricots and chop them finely, then stir these and the nuts (if using) and breadcrumbs into the meat mixture. Divide between individual ovenproof dishes (it will serve up to four) and press down firmly. Mix together the milk and dried milk and beat in the egg and egg yolk (if using). Pour over the meat in each dish. Stand the pots on a baking sheet and bake at gas mark 5, 375°F (190°C) for 30 minutes or until the egg topping has set. Serve hot.

Sorbets

Using the basic sugar syrup (p.91) blend equal amounts of this syrup with a chosen fruit purée, whatever is in season. Freeze for an hour or two until the edges are frozen but the centre is still slushy. Turn into a bowl and beat until smooth. For each half pint (300ml) beat 1 egg white until stiff and then fold it in. Cover and freeze until firm. Just before the meal, scoop into a serving dish and keep in the top of the fridge until you are ready to serve.

Apple and honey sorbet
Blend equal quantities of sugar syrup and apple purée and stir in enough honey to flavour the mixture. Freeze and continue as above.

Lemon sorbet
Add the grated rind and juice of 2 lemons to each half pint (300ml) of sugar syrup. Freeze and continue as above.

Tomato sorbet
This between-course savoury sorbet doesn't need sugar. All you do is mix together the puréed and sieved contents of a can of tomatoes (14oz/400g) with the juice of ½ a

lemon and a dash of brown sauce. Freeze until slushy, then fold in 1 stiffly beaten egg white. Freeze and serve as above.

Frozen Lemon Sponge   *Makes enough for 4*

2oz (50g) thick yogurt
4oz (125g) butter
6oz (175g) sugar
3 eggs, separated
1 lemon
Cooked sponge cake (see p.85)

Cream the butter and sugar together and fold in the egg yolks, yogurt and grated rind and juice of the lemon. Beat the egg whites until stiff and then fold into the egg yolk mixture. Line the base of a large loaf tin with sponge cake and top with the lemon mixture. Cover with sponge cake. Freeze and serve in slices.

Beignets de bananes
Although you could use ordinary thick pancake batter for this dish I prefer this very crispy variation which uses the white of an egg.

3 rounded tablespoons flour
1 dessertspoon sunflower oil
Warm water
1 egg white
1 banana
Oil for frying

Mix together the flour and the oil with enough warm water to make a smooth thick paste. Leave to stand for at least 1 hour. Just before using, whisk the egg white until stiff and fold into the mixture.

   Halve the banana, then cut each half in 2 lengthways to

get 4 pieces. Dip each piece into the batter and fry in very hot oil. Drain on kitchen paper. Serve on a hot plate.

☆ *Left-over batter can be deep-fried until crisp and sprinkled with sugar or salt for 'nibbles'.*

Dried fruit compote

2 teaspoons honey
1/2 teaspoon dried ginger
4fl oz (125ml) orange juice
3oz (75g) mixed dried fruit
(prune, apricot, pear, apple, etc.)
Thick yogurt

Blend together the honey, ginger and the orange juice and pour over the dried fruits. Leave to soak overnight.

Put into a pan and simmer for 10 minutes. Serve hot or cold with cream, thick yogurt or Sweet yogurt dressing (p.49).

☆ *Keep a carton of long-life double cream in stock for entertaining emergencies.*

☆ *Wine is expensive to buy by the bottle as it is always too much for one, sometimes even too much for two. Consider the economics of buying the small cartons (packed in threes) which each hold two glasses. Left-over wine can be added to a casserole or blended with vinegar to make your own wine vinegar.*

☆ *An ideal way to make the most of a few dried apricots and left-over white wine is to put them together. Apricots soaked in wine keep for ages. I have a Kilner jar in constant use which I top up with dried apricots and wine as they come to hand. Eat on their own as a yummy dessert or together with ice-cream, or in any recipe which calls for soaked dried apricots.*

119

6
AND THERE'S MORE . . .

When you live on your own, are unemployed or on a pension it's often very difficult to fix a set allowance for food. What happens when a severe winter brings forth high fuel bills? We have to rob Peter to pay Paul. Just when we most need nourishing warming foods we can least afford them.

Self-sufficiency

When you can harvest your own crops, use your own fresh herbs, take advantage of Nature's bounty and, above all, be your own 'manufacturer', then money will go much further. This is why it is important to grab opportunities to do what you can and put the money saved aside for that rainy day. This type of saving is above and beyond the normal money you can save by careful shopping and imaginative cooking as shown in the four-week Challenge.

The way to do it is this. Every time you can grow or make something that you might normally have bought, then don't count it as 'free'. Pay for it in the normal way. Role-play the shopkeeper. Put the money in the 'till' and the weekly savings in the bank. Then it can gain interest.

Make your own marmalade

For speed I use the ready-prepared marmalade oranges in tins. Using 2 × 2.1lb (1kg) bags of sugar this makes 7lb (3.5kg). Cost: £1.44p, so approximately 20p per lb (500g). Compare this with the price of the shop marmalade. Even allowing for fuel and jam-pot covers you can expect to save 10p per lb/500g.

One for the pot

You don't need an allotment to start growing things. I have beans in barrels and peas in pots. Most of my produce I grow in pots. This way you get just enough at any one time for one person.

It really *is* worth taking the trouble to grow what you can because you won't buy anything fresher. Even the top restaurants can't beat that. But seeds are not cheap and there are often too many in a packet for one person. Use some of these ideas for getting value for money:

- Share seeds with friends. Let Cynthia buy the lettuce seeds, you the cabbage.
- Sow a few seeds each week to get a continuous crop. Exchange spare seedlings.
- If space is limited grow the cut-and-come again varieties such as the lettuce called Salad Bowl. Pick off only the leaves you need. New ones grow.
- Grow red-leaved lettuce alongside the green to add colour and class to your salads.
- When runner beans have finished cropping cut off at ground level and leave the roots in the soil. These will shoot again the following year.
- Try to save a few seeds from your own plants each year. This not only saves you having to buy new seeds but gives the plant – through successive generations – a chance to become acclimatised to your own garden conditions. This gives it a fighting chance against the weeds which flourish because they've been around for decades.

☆ *Wrap left-over seeds tightly in foil and keep in the fridge. Remember to label! Most seeds remain viable for several years when kept in cool conditions.*

One weed that is worth cultivating is the *dandelion*. This is the most versatile of plants. I've used the flower petals for wine, the milky sap as a 'glue', the leaves for salads and the roots as a coffee substitute. Because I have to take everything to its limit I've even sprayed the 'clocks' with hair lacquer to use in a flower arrangement.

Dandelion coffee
Dandelion coffee is well known as an agreeable substitute for the 'real' thing. Some people can't tell the difference. But why not make up a blend of both? It's a good way of making your expensive coffee grounds go further.

Dig up the roots in the late autumn. Scrub clean and pat dry in a towel. Leave to dry out thoroughly, preferably in a sunny spot. Roast the dried roots in a moderate oven (gas mark 4, 350°F, 180°C) until they are brittle. Crush with a rolling pin, pestle and mortar or (better) give a quick whizz in a grinder. Use as normal ground coffee.

Pick of the crops
We need vitamins and minerals to maintain a healthy body and the very best way to get these is through a *varied* diet of fruits and vegetables. I know that, you know that, but how often do we stick to buying the same old things just out of habit?

Recently I've discovered that some vegetables and fruits are particularly well worth eating (and not always the bits you expect), so now I'm becoming a little more adventurous and hope you will do too.

Beetroot:
Here's a surprise. The leaves contain more goodness than the roots, and are on a par with spinach. Worth growing as you can't get this part in the shops. Simmer the leaves in very little water until tender. Serve as a vegetable with meat.

Broccoli:
Best of the greens. Rich in iron, calcium and all vitamins.

Brussels sprouts:
One of the best of the winter crops containing all the essential vitamins and mineral salts.

Cabbage:
Low in vitamins compared to other greens but worth eating because of its high fibre content.

Carrots:
High in vitamin A which is good for your eyesight.

Kale:
This valuable vegetable has loads of fibre and all the B vitamins, also some vitamin A. Rich in protein and mineral salts too it grows well in any garden.

Leeks (also Onions):
Claimed to be one of the most nourishing vegetables. Good for colds and for keeping a clear skin.

Mushrooms:
I discovered these to be one of the most important foods with plenty of minerals and vitamins plus other useful attributes. I grow my own mushrooms indoors in normal (but not bright) light using one of the boxed kits. These cost around £3 and will crop up to 6lb (3kg) of mushrooms over several weeks, i.e. less than half the price of shop-bought mushrooms.
To cook mushrooms: Avoid frying. This adds enormously to their calorie content. Instead, heat them through by pouring over boiling water and leaving them to stand for a few minutes. Do this anyway before frying as they then won't take up so much fat. Don't forget that raw mushrooms are delicious. Just wipe clean (no need to peel), slice and toss in a little salad dressing.

Mustard and Cress:
By this I mean the kind we grow on flannels, not the commercial boxed variety which is something else. Very rich in vitamins and minerals, it is worthy of more attention than just as a garnish.

Radishes:
I use to spend hours carving these up into 'roses' which open up after a few hours' soak in iced water, never believing them to be of much more use than to pretty up a dish. Now I've discovered they are very rich in iron, calcium, potassium and iodine. What's more they are well endowed with vitamins, so I've stopped carving and started chewing.

Chopped radish *leaves* with their sharp, almost watercress flavour make a good addition to a salad.

Sprouting seeds:
These are nature's little miracles and the very best, quickest and easiest way to get those essential vitamins and minerals. You don't even need to step outside. Most people now are familiar with the mung bean shoots which are often used in Chinese cooking, but for all round goodness you can't beat alfalfa. Just listen to this: alfalfa sprouts are high in vitamins A, B, B complex, C, D, E, K and U and also contain calcium, iron, phosphorus, magnesium, potassium, sodium, silicone, chlorine, aluminium and sulphur. What's more they have a very high protein content! In particular the vitamin C content increases about 1000 per cent within 4 days of sprouting and it is said that one teacupful of these sprouts will contain as much vitamin C as ten glasses of pure orange juice.

Salad alfalfa can be bought from seed merchants and some health food shops and one packet lasts quite a time. Directions for growing are on the packet. Briefly, all you do is put about 1 dessertspoon of seeds in a glass jar or tumbler together with some tepid water. Cover the glass with muslin and secure with a rubber band (these are sometimes included in the packet). Shake well and drain off the water. Repeat twice a day for 3–6 days by which time they will be ready to eat. They grow anywhere (dark or light) as long as the temperature is warm. Add to salads or include in sandwiches.

Swede:
This is a must for winter casseroles being one of the richest in the B vitamins and it also contains other vitamins and minerals.

Turnips:
Grow these yourself because turnip tops are a valuable food as well as the roots being rich in iron and calcium. They also have a high vitamin A content.

Watercress:
Contains vitamins A, C and E, also iron and sulphur so worth eating as often as possible. Use the leaves for salads and stems for soups. Keep fresh by plunging the *leaves* (not the stems) in water.

Braised beetroot

If you can't get hold of the leaves, here is a lovely way of cooking the beets. Although this recipe is designed for hob-top cooking, once you reach the seasoning stage it could be completed by cooking in the oven. As always it all depends on your plan for the day.

1 tablespoon sunflower oil
½ onion, sliced
1 beetroot, peeled and thinly sliced
1 teaspoon flour
1 dessertspoon vinegar
3fl oz (75ml) water or beef stock
Pepper to taste

Heat the oil in a frying-pan and gently cook the onions until transparent. Add the beetroot and cook until the onions are golden.

Sprinkle in the flour and stir, turning the vegetables in the flour until it turns brown. Blend the vinegar with the water, add to the vegetables and stir until it begins to thicken. Season with pepper to taste.

Cover the pan and leave over a low heat for 20–30 minutes or until the beetroot is tender.

Swede-ish soufflé

Said to be wonderful served with turkey or wild game, this recipe is also delicious with my more mundane chicken. It is equally good made with turnips.

8oz (250g) swede
1oz (25g) butter
1 teaspoon sugar
1 slice bread, crumbled
1 egg, separated

Peel the swede and grate it (or chop in a food processor). Mix with the remaining ingredients except the egg white.

Beat the egg white until it forms peaks and fold into the swede mixture. Transfer to a 1 pint (600ml) greased soufflé dish and bake in a pre-heated oven for 30 minutes at gas mark 4, 350°F (180°C) until the top is golden.

Herbs

Everyone should grow a few herbs, either in the garden or on a sunny windowsill. Herbs add so much flavour that they can transform the most boring and economical dish into something fit for a king. They can be used fresh or dried but the time at which you dry them is critical to obtain the maximum flavour. A general rule is that:

- In early summer, before the flowers appear, the flavour is in the leaf.
- In mid-summer and early autumn the flavour is more pronounced in the stem.
- In late autumn and winter concentration is in the roots.

So early summer is usually the best time to dry your herbs.

Which herbs to grow?
This has to be according to your personal taste and it's far better to grow a small selection of the herbs you like and will use than clumps and clumps of things you won't. But don't be afraid to experiment: try one herb with different meats and one meat with different herbs.

Happy herb combinations

	Lamb	Beef	Poultry	Pork	Fish	Eggs	Cheese	Vegetables
Basil			■	■	■	■	■	■
Bay			■			■		
Chives						■	■	
Rosemary	■					■		■
Parsley		■	■		■	■		■
Mint	■					■	■	■
Thyme	■	■	■	■	■			
Sage			■	■			■	■
Marjoram		■	■		■			■
Fennel					■	■		
Garlic	■	■				■		

Courgette in tomato and thyme sauce

One courgette is exactly the right amount for one person.
Use this recipe as a substantial starter or serve as a
vegetable to accompany your main course.

---

1 courgette
1/2oz (15g) butter
1/2 teaspoon chopped fresh thyme, or a pinch of dried thyme
1 tinned tomato with 1 tablespoon of juice
Pepper to taste

Thinly slice the courgette. Melt the butter in a small pan,
add the courgette and the thyme and fry gently for one
minute. Chop the tomato and add this, with the juice, to
the pan. Simmer gently until the sauce has thickened
slightly and the courgette is tender. Season with pepper.
Serve hot.

Herb stuffing

This traditional stuffing is far superior to the packet stuff.
Ring the changes by serving as a topping instead of mashed
potato when making a cottage pie. Vary the herb
according to the meat of the day.

1/2oz (15g) butter
1 dessertspoon grated onion
1 slice brown bread, crumbed
Pepper to taste
1 teaspoon grated lemon rind (optional)
1 tablespoon chopped fresh herbs, or 1 teaspoon dried herbs
1/2 beaten egg (2 tablespoons – see p.25)

Melt the butter in a small pan and gently fry the onion.
Turn out the heat and add the rest of the ingredients.
Blend well. If too dry, moisten with a few drops of water.
Use as directed in your chosen recipe (e.g. Marrow flower
fritters, p.131).

☆ *Fresh breadcrumbs absorb more flavour if they are allowed to dry out slightly before use. After making the crumbs, spread on a baking sheet and leave to stand uncovered for at least 1 hour before using.*

Herb oils and vinegars

These are wonderfully aromatic and just the job for salad dressings and marinades. They also make good presents. Make in small quantities so that you have a large selection.

Oils

Best with basil, rosemary or thyme. You need 1 tablespoon roughly chopped herbs to each 5fl oz (150ml) sunflower oil. Add the herbs to the oil and stir in 2 teaspoons vinegar. Pour into a small bottle and seal. Leave in a sunny place. Shake the bottle every day and after a month strain off the oil into a fresh jar. Repeat if you need more flavour.

Vinegars

For this leave the herb leaves intact. Basil, mint, thyme and tarragon seem to work best. Fill a wide-mouthed screw-top jar with loosely packed herbs and cover with vinegar (any sort). Screw on the lid and shake the jar every day. Taste after two weeks. For a more concentrated flavour strain the liquid over a fresh batch of leaves and repeat. Finally, strain into a clean bottle and pop in a sprig of the herb used for effect.

Home-made liqueurs

Home-made liqueurs are a real luxury without being too expensive. Buy the cheapest brandy to make them and offset this expense by giving away some of the 'goodies' as presents. Some people drain off the liqueur and re-bottle it for drinking, but I like to leave the fruit steeping and drain off only what I (we) need to drink at the time. The fruit can be used in sweet or savoury dishes. For example, steeped orange shreds are delicious as a garnish for white fish or sprinkled over ice cream. Also, try including a spoonful in a beef casserole.

I use steeped black cherries in steamed puddings or to make miniature Black Forest Gateaux. They mix well into a fresh or dried fruit salad (see p.119) and make a good filling for pancakes too.

Method
Prepare the fruit according to type (see below) and then put it in clean screw-top jars with the required amount of sugar and brandy. Seal and shake to dissolve the sugar, then store in a cool dark place for at least 8 weeks before using. Shake the bottles twice a week (I pin up a note to remind me) for maximum flavour.

For orange liqueur:
Combine the juice and rind of 1 large orange, 2oz (50g) caster sugar and 10fl oz (300ml) brandy. Be sure to remove all the pith and shred the orange rind very finely.

For cherry liqueur:
Combine 8oz (250g) stoned black cherries, 4oz (125g) caster sugar and 10fl oz (300ml) brandy. Prick the cherries with a darning needle before putting them in the jar.

Flower power
Many flowers can be used for culinary purposes and I have one or two favourites that I keep especially for that purpose. They also look good growing either in the garden or in pots on your windowsills.

Pot marigold:
The brilliant orange petals can be used fresh or dried. Scatter over salads or infuse in soups such as carrot soup

to give a deep rich colour that only the expensive saffron can match. You can also infuse them in water, then strain this and use it for cooking rice for Kedgeree (p.39) or rice salad.

Nasturtium:
I start off the seeds in small (yogurt) pots and later transfer them to their final position (usually in old buckets). The leaves contain iron, calcium and vitamins C and E and are a delicious addition to any salad. Gather the seeds to pickle for mock capers: pick while still green, put the seeds in a jar and cover with cooled, boiled vinegar. Store in the dark and give them a couple of months to mature before using in 'caper' sauce.

Rose:
My favourite. The dark reds I gather for Rose petal jam (p.132) and the other blooms when full blown are dried to make pot-pourri.

Marrow flower fritters
Anyone who grows marrows or courgettes knows only too well that there is an abundance of male flowers maturing before the females arrive. Why not use these to enhance your main meal?

---

2 or 4 marrow flowers
About 4oz herb stuffing (see p.128)
Sunflower oil for deep-frying
About 5fl oz (150ml) fritter batter (see Beignets de bananes, p.118

Fill each flower with the herb stuffing, folding the ends of the petals over to make a parcel.

Heat the oil. Dip each flower parcel into the batter and drop carefully into the oil. When crisp and golden remove and drain well on kitchen paper. Serve hot.

Rose petal jam

You need at least 10 large roses to each 1lb of sugar, preferably a dark red variety (although you can add a drop of food colouring if all you have is pink) and – of course – sweetly scented.

Cut off all the white ends of the rose petals to prevent bitterness. Dissolve 1lb (500g) sugar in 7fl oz (200ml) water, add the juice of ½ small lemon and all the rose petals. Simmer until the petals look glossy, crystallised and the jam has thickened. Keep stirring to prevent burning and don't overcook or the petals become tough. Pot as for jam in the usual way or strain to get rose petal jelly.

Rose petal water ice

8oz (250g) sugar
1 pint (600ml) water
1 teaspoon grated lemon rind
Juice of 1 lemon
1 tablespoon rose petal jelly

Dissolve the sugar in the water and stir in the rest of the ingredients. Bring to the boil. Allow to cool, then freeze. When the mixture is slushy, remove from the freezer and beat well to incorporate air. Re-freeze.

Fruit for free

Unless you grow fruit in the garden you haven't much option other than to pay for it. All fruits are good, blackcurrants being particularly high in vitamin C. But one of the best hedgerow fruits is the blackberry which contains calcium, iron and phosphorus. With loads of vitamin C and all the B vitamins too it's well worth cultivating if you do have a garden. Otherwise try to take the opportunity to get into the countryside and pick them.

Blackberry cordial

1 pint (600ml) white vinegar
1 ½–2lb (750–1kg) blackberries
1 lb (500g) sugar
8oz (250g) honey

Pour the vinegar over the berries and leave to stand for one week, stirring and pressing the fruit every day to extract the maximum amount of juice. Strain the liquid into a pan and add the sugar and honey. Bring slowly to the boil, stir, then boil for five minutes. Allow to cool. Store in sterilised bottles sealed with screw-tops or corks and keep in a cool dark place.

Use 1 tablespoon of the cordial stirred into 1 glass of hot water for a bedtime drink. This is also a traditional winter drink for colds and sore throats.

Blackberry butter
Delicious spread on scones, I make this with the windfall apples but almost any crisp green apple would do.

1 lb (500g) green apples
1 lemon
1 lb (500g) blackberries
12oz (350g) sugar to each 1 lb (500g) fruit pulp (see below)

Chop up the apples *including* the skins and cores. Place in a saucepan with the juice and rind of the lemon. Add the blackberries and simmer the lot together gently for about 15 minutes or until really soft. Rub through a sieve to extract skin and pips.

Weigh the pulp and add the correct proportion of sugar. Heat until the sugar has dissolved, then boil for 15–20 minutes until thick, stirring often. Pot into small sterilised jars, cover, cool and keep in the fridge.

7
OVER TO YOU

I never believe that I know everything, so it was important to me to find out what other single folk would make of my plan. Hilda (a senior citizen), Ruth (a single parent), Joan (a working girl) and Lynda (a student) were all asked to have a go at using my approach, then tell me what they thought.

The Senior Citizen

Hilda agreed that writing down what she bought highlighted areas in her diet that needed re-thinking but pointed out that 'it is extremely difficult to change old habits'. (I find it hard too!) She felt that as she got older she needed less food, but I think older people need to be particularly careful not to neglect their diet.

Hilda's main weakness was that she spent 'far too much on cakes and biscuits and ought to transfer some of that amount to fruit and the amount I spend on tinned meat to fresh meat' so that she would then 'have a better diet with more variety'. There's nothing like a bit of analysis with pen and paper to point up how you can improve your lot.

The Single Parent

Ruth has a little boy of three and previously had not been interested in cooking. She told me that 'mealtimes became a real drag because convenience foods were boring'.

The Challenge proved to Ruth that by doing her own thing she could become more interested in preparing meals and actually enjoy being able to 'produce the sort of meals I was proud to serve to my son. For the first time since he was a baby he ate all that was put in front of him at mealtimes and he took great interest in the food during and after preparation'.

Shopping became *'fun and an exploration'* as Ruth walked down the supermarket aisles seeking out bargains and *'getting very strange looks while I shook tins of beans to see which had less sauce'*. By looking more closely at prices she discovered that some 'cheap' packs (she quoted meat as an example) were not always as money-saving as they seemed at first sight. After a couple of weeks she said *'I became very confident at asking the shopkeeper to sell me 6oz of cabbage (instead of a whole one) or exactly 70p worth of cheese.'* The money went further and instead of *'serving 2 or 3 mundane basic meals a day'* Ruth could *'now provide 4 good meals a day for the same cost'*.

When you eat good food you feel a lot better – I've found that out for myself. I'm glad to say Ruth found the same: *'I felt a lot healthier than I had in a long time and instead of lolling around lazily I was full of "get up and go". Most of all I stopped nibbling between meals.'*

The Working Girl

Joan is a perfect example of what you can do if you put your mind to it. She has an extremely full life so has perfected a routine which means she doesn't have to slave away in her kitchen and yet she manages to produce interesting meals.

'I'm perfectly capable of processing my own food' says Joan, *'so why pay someone else to do it for me and take away many of the valuable nutrients?'* (Hear, hear!) So it goes without saying that Joan avoids convenience foods.

Time is at a premium for full-time workers so she organises herself well. *'Two tasks are done at the same time: for example, when waiting for bread to rise, other dishes will be prepared to cook in the oven at the same time.'*

But it can still be hard work and, in particular, *'Eating alone when you are young and single can be deathly'* says Joan. She agrees with me that company is important: *'At least once a week I try to include eating with a friend. A shared bottle of wine is usually a fair exchange for a shared meal.'*

Joan aims to shop once a week and has found out that *'fruit works out an inexpensive way of staving off hunger pangs'*. (A good tip for Hilda!) *'Shopping at a market is an enjoyable way of buying produce and at the end of a day's trading fruit and vegetables are often sold at greatly reduced prices. Expensive delights such as avocado pears, grapes and mushrooms can be sold at give-away prices.'*

Joan's tips for saving:

Home-made bread gives two savings: first on cost and second on taking lunch to work rather than buying when there.

Porridge is one of the best traditional breakfasts. You can't beat it on value for money or nutrition.

Dry kidney beans are half the price of canned. Soak and cook in bulk, then freeze.

The Student

Lynda expected my Rule of Four to be *'a rather long and laborious process of working out calories, kilojoules and vitamin and fibre intake'* but instead found *'it is a very easy, yet effective device'*.

Chicken she discovered to be *'excellent value for money'* making *'roast chicken, chicken salad and 3 chicken and sweetcorn flans – plus the carcass for soup – all from one 3lb 14oz bird'*. I'm impressed – because good use was made of that chicken. If there was a problem it was that by buying a whole bird she didn't have any money left over for more variety in the meat line. But as Lynda said *'I'm lucky, I had the facility of a freezer so I could freeze unused meat and the flans'*, so it didn't have to be eaten up within a few days.

Lynda realised the value of vegetable protein in a low-budget diet but did buy it ready-cooked in cans (red kidney beans, butter beans, etc). With access to a freezer and following Joan's advice she could save money by cooking her own pulses.

Like me, Lynda found that once she had built up a storecupboard of the basic items: salt, pepper, herbs, etc. she could then buy what what was value for money and nothing else – for example, larger jars of coffee or bags of flour instead of the smallest sizes. Once she had these she said *'I could divide my money into 4 and know that I wouldn't have to spend most of my allocated grocery money on odds and ends but could buy actual food and at the same time have a healthy and nutritionally balanced diet.'*

Can I have the Last Word . . .?

What began as an experiment into the economics of cooking for one has led me, via various routes, to a far greater understanding of the food we eat and what it does for us and to us.

Being poor should never mean that the fun goes out of cooking. In fact it can be the reverse. Think positive. A lack of money makes you think more carefully about what you're buying and whether it's worth it – and that's actually a *good* thing. Not only that, but by going back to home cooking you get the bonus of a healthier diet giving you loads of 'get up and go' (as Ruth discovered). And if, like me, you lose countless battles over endless years trying to fight the flab, then try my approach to The Challenge. I gave up diets during that time and actually ate more than I do usually. But it was all good sensible stuff and, unbelievably, the weight slowly started to decrease and has continued to do so.

Physically, mentally and financially I'm better off. Too Goode to be True? Well, prove me wrong. Now there's a challenge for you!

BOOKLIST

GENDERS, R. *Grow your own health foods* Foulsham, pbk, 1983.

HASELGROVE, N. M. and SCALLON, K. A. *The how and why of cookery* Collins, 4th rev. edn, 1985.

LONGMATE, N. *How we lived then: a history of everyday life during the Second World War* Hutchinson, 1971. op; Arrow Books, 1977. op.

MINISTRY OF AGRICULTURE, FISHERIES AND FOOD *Manual of nutrition* HMSO, 8th edn, 1976.

PEMBER REEVES, M. *Round about a pound a week* Virago, new edn of 1915 edn, pbk, 1979.

RAY, E. *The resourceful cook, or what to cook when there's nothing to cook* Macmillan, 1978. op.

SPRING RICE, M. *Working class wives* Virago, new edn, pbk, 1981.

STOBART, T. *The cook's encyclopaedia: ingredients and processes* Batsford, 1980. op; Macmillan, pbk, 1981. op.

INDEX

Conversion tables

All the conversions used in this book are *approximate* conversions, which have either been rounded up or down. In a few recipes it has been necessary to modify them very slightly. Never mix metric and imperial measures in one recipe. Stick to one system or the other.

Weights		Volume		Measurements	
½oz	15g	1 fl oz	25ml	¼ inch	0·5cm
1	25	2	50	½	1
1½	40	3	75	1	2·5
2	50	5 (¼ pint)	150	2	5
3	75	10 (½)	300	3	7·5
4	125	15 (¾)	450	4	10
5	150	1 pint	600	6	15
6	175	1¼	750	7	18
7	200	1½	900	8	20·5
8	250	1¾	1 litre	9	23
9	275	2	1·1	11	28
10	300	2¼	1·3	12	30·5
12	350	2½	1·4		
13	375	2¾	1·6	**Oven temp.**	
14	400	3	1·7	Mk 1 275°F 140°C	
15	425	3¼	2·8	2 300 150	
1lb	500	3½	2	3 325 170	
1¼	625	3¾	2·1	4 350 180	
1½	750	4	2·3	5 375 190	
2	1 kg	5	2·8	6 400 200	
3	1·5	6	3·4	7 425 220	
4	2	7	4·0	8 450 230	
5	2·5	8 (1 gal)	4·5	9 475 240	

Imperial spoon measures have been used in many recipes. These are *level* spoonfuls unless otherwise stated. If you prefer to work in metric, use the following equivalents:

teaspoon	=	5ml measuring spoon
dessertspoon	=	10ml measuring spoon
tablespoon	=	15ml measuring spoon

GOODE FOR ONE

SHIRLEY GOODE

BBC BOOKS

This book includes recipes featured in the
BBC Television series *Bazaar* first broadcast
on BBC 1 from January 1987. The series was
produced by Erica Griffiths.

Published to accompany a series of programmes
prepared in consultation with the BBC Continuing
Education Advisory Council.

Cover photographs by S. Jeffrey Binns,
Ivanhoe Studios Ltd

Published by BBC Books,
a division of BBC Enterprises Ltd
35 Marylebone High Street, London W1M 4AA

First published 1987
© Shirley Goode 1987
ISBN 0 563 21326 4

This book is set in 10/11pt Gill Light
Photoset on Linotron 202 by
Rowland Phototypesetting,
Bury St Edmunds,
England
Printed by Richard Clay Ltd,
Bungay, England.